MW01379926

Walter Keller is the founder and owner of the Lumber Baron Inn. Here he plays the role of police officer Rusty Schwinn amidst the hubbub of a mystery dinner in the ballroom of the mansion.

The Lumber Baron Inn: Denver's Mystery Mansion

By Phil Goodstein

Denver

New Social Publications

2013

To Carl Schmidt:
The owner of the Capitol Hill Mansion
who has been a most accommodating host
for an itinerant tour guide

Walter Keller designed the cover.
The back cover photo is by Tom Torgove.

The Lumber Baron Inn: Denver's Mystery Mansion

New Social Publications
Box 18026; Denver, Colorado 80218
(303)333-1095
capitolhillbooks.com for information about books
from New Social Publications
lumberbaron.com for information about the Lumber Baron Inn

Printed in Denver, Colorado
First Edition: November 2013

Library of Congress Control Number 2013915259
ISBN 0–9742264–9–1

Contents

The John Mouat Mansion, at the northeast corner of West 37th Avenue, has become the Lumber Baron Inn. The above shot shows how it looked in 1912 compared to the bottom picture of the structure one hundred years later.

Foreword
By Walter Keller

From the moment I entered the John Mouat Mansion in 1991, I dreamed of a book that solved its many mysteries. Wandering around its grand interior, which features craftsmanship from a bygone era, I imagined this volume revealing the nature of who constructed it and why it was built. The pages would map the mansion's opulent beginnings, when its owners were bursting with hope, through its harrowing crash into condemnation and abandonment. I saw the pages featuring photos of the many characters associated with the house and its architectural evolution. This unwritten book in my mind was to answer every last question anyone might pose who visited the imposing three-story brick and stone structure. Such a book did not exist in the early months when I acquired the landmark. Not surprisingly, it still does not exist.

The very fantasy of such a comprehensive history spoke more to my youthful naiveté than to the realities of why or who would write such a volume. Do not all great landmarks eventually have a study written about them? The answer, of course, is no. Many vanish leaving few traces. But over two decades later, I find myself on the brink of publishing my best attempt to fulfill that dream.

The reasons for its production seem more complex to me today than my simple vision of years ago. As much as ever, I relish having the answers to the many mysteries associated with the house. In this sense, writing this book has a simple aim. But now, with so much time passed living and working in the building, this volume also sets forth certain facts stripping away much of the misinformation and misunderstandings about the place. It aims to memorialize the fruitful labor of all who helped save a Denver jewel from near demolition. With a glance towards the future, it hopes to inspire further research that might one day meet those youthful expectations of my first visit.

Naturally then, writing even a less-than-comprehensive history of this Victorian manor has proven challenging. This is a reason why even grander buildings

The Mouat Mansion is on the left in this 1922 shot of the intersection of West 37th Avenue and Bryant Street.

never get histories written about them. Tremendous amounts of work, diligence, and organization are just the beginning of such a pursuit. The following pages represent that tedious process.

Hitting the 20-year milestone of owning the mansion a couple of years ago helped shock me from simple information compilation into publication. Just one additional bed and breakfast guest with a gnawing, quizzical look upon departure additionally pushed me finally to create a book to help satisfy their curiosity. For years I threatened anyone who would listen, that I myself would pen such a story. This boast never took into account either my enormously time-filled schedule or, perhaps, my lack of discipline and writing skills for such an assignment. Fortunately, I have become friends with Denver's most colorful historian, Phil Goodstein. In Phil, I discovered the perfect match for my current unfulfilled literary ambitions who has further helped me open the doors of the Lumber Baron Inn to assure its central part in the city's past, present, and future.

Lumber Baron Inn

What the Mouat Mansion looked like when Walter Keller acquired it on April 1, 1991.

Potter Highlands

Located at the northeast corner of West 37th Avenue and Bryant Street, the Lumber Baron Inn is the dominating house in Potter Highlands. This is the subdivision covering the half mile between West 32nd and West 38th avenues and the half mile from Zuni Street to Federal Boulevard. The neighborhood and the house embody Denver. Both are products of the early growth of the Mile High City and 19th-century suburban dreams.

On November 16, 1858, William Larimer, a veteran town founder, arrived at the confluence of Cherry Creek and the Platte River with the intention of creating a trade city in the center of the nascent Pikes Peak gold rush—the Pikes Peak region was anywhere within a couple of hundred miles of the mountain. Larimer found that prospectors from Georgia had already laid out the city of gold, Auraria, on the southwest bank of Cherry Creek. At the end of the day on which he arrived, around midnight on November 16–17, Larimer forded Cherry Creek. Seeing no settlement on the other side of the stream, he claimed the land as Denver City. The name honored James W. Denver, the governor of Kansas Territory who had authorized Larimer to create a government for Arapahoe County. This was the portion of Kansas Territory west of the current Colorado-Kansas boundary. Prior to the Pikes Peak enthusiasm, Kansas authorities had not imposed their authority there since the land was reserved for Indians and had a minuscule white population.

As Larimer was well aware, Charles Nichols and members of what was known as the Lawrence party had previously staked claim to the northeast bank of Cherry Creek, the location of modern downtown. They had christened it St. Charles, Kansas Territory, for Nichols' home town of St. Charles, Missouri. Nichols and associates had left it in charge of William McGaa, the dissolute son of a British noble lord who had run away to sea as a youth and was living with the Arapaho Indians at the time of the Pikes Peak gold rush. Members of the St. Charles Town Company had gone back to Kansas to file their claim and get supplies for what they were sure would be a deluge of prospectors in the spring of 1859.

Walter McDuffie Potter is the namesake of Potter Highlands.

Far from watching after the interests of St. Charles, McGaa joined Larimer in creating Denver City. Even as he sought to build an instant community, Larimer realized that Nichols and associates might ultimately gain legal possession of the real estate. To protect himself from this possibility, on December 11, 1858, Larimer preempted the land across the Platte River as Highland. It was his fallback in case the authorities upheld the Lawrence party. Larimer staked the spread all the way to the equivalent of West 26th Avenue and Zuni Street.

While Nichols gained official Kansas recognition of the St. Charles site, that did him little good. When he returned to the confluence of Cherry Creek and the Platte in early 1859, he was met by Larimer and others who had since become part of the Denver City Town Company. They gave Nichols the choice between accepting a few lots in the settlement in exchange for his deed or a piece of rope around his neck. He chose the former, quickly selling the property and leaving the region.

On this basis, Denver, Auraria, and Highland grew into a community of 4,749 people by the time of the 1860 census. Already on December 3, 1859, residents had merged into greater Denver. They chose the name Denver since that tiny settlement was the site of the stagecoach stop to which all mail and passengers arrived. Merger was necessary to protect all three communities from the possibility that a rival town, especially Golden, might emerge as the commanding trade metropolis of the Pikes Peak region. The agreement designated Auraria, the land the other side of Cherry Creek, as West Denver; the old Denver City, downtown proper, became East Denver; everything on the other side of the Platte River—Highland—was North Denver. A South Denver, mostly to the south of Sixth Avenue and the other side of Cherry Creek, did not emerge until the 1880s.

After an initial burst of enthusiasm, when upwards of 100,000 people headed toward the future Colorado in 1859–61, development stagnated with the playing out of the initial gold fields and the advent of the Civil War. During the middle of the 1860s, Denver's population slumped to little more than 3,000. Even so, dreamers and speculators continued to believe the city was ideally posed for future growth. They filed claims to land considerably beyond Denver's original borders of Colfax Avenue on the south, Broadway on the east, Zuni Street on the west, and the equivalent of 26th Avenue on the north.

Walter McDuffie Potter was among those who were sure Denver would quickly grow. A young Baptist missionary, he arrived in the nascent Mile High City in 1863 in the hope of recovering his health. This was another theme of early Denver. Besides gold, the community claimed to have a most salubrious climate. All people had to do to recover from tuberculosis and other deadly lung ailments, promoters insisted, was to come to the high, dry climate and breathe in the marvelous air. Before World War I, anywhere between 20 and 50 percent of the people making Colorado their home did so for health considerations.

The American Baptist Home Mission Society assisted Potter in relocating to Denver. It instructed him to create an organized Baptist religious presence in Colorado. On December 27, 1863, the preacher hosted a meeting that led to the founding of First Baptist Church on May 2 of the next year. Simultaneously, Potter hoped to enrich himself and support the church through land investments.

In collaboration with his sister, Lucy K. Potter, the evangelist preempted the spread just to the northwest of early Highland in 1864, property which became Potter Highlands. He envisaged it as an idyllic development with pristine air that would allow him and others suffering from poor health to recover from their maladies while the profits it generated would enhance the work of the church. Despite such a glowing ideal, his health continued to decline. By late 1865, both his physical well-being and finances were in dire straits when he returned East. Potter died the next year at age 29.

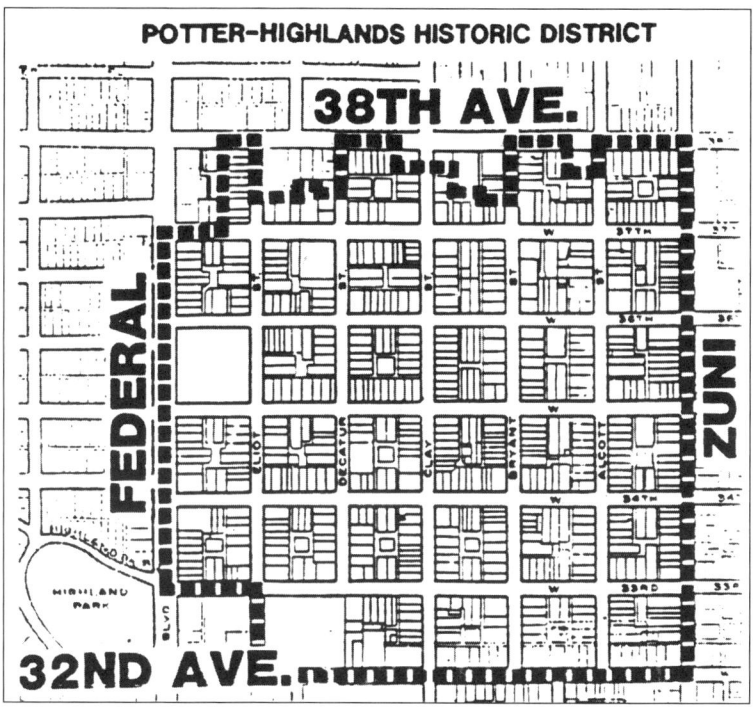

Potter Highlands Preservation Association

Most of Potter Highlands is in a landmark district.

On November 11, 1865, Potter had made out his will. He specified all of his personal holdings were to go to Lucy. The real estate was to pass to the American Baptist Home Mission Society. She married Ezra Humphrey on April 16, 1868. By this time, there were disputes between her family and the Baptists about who owned Potter Highlands. Not until 1880 did they reach an agreement when Ezra Humphrey arranged for the Baptists to receive all of the remaining land from the estate of his wife's brother.

Development was then rapidly underway on the spread. Promoters filed the first plat for the area on July 8, 1873. Both the Baptists and the Potter family wanted Potter Highlands because they were convinced of Denver's great future. Simultaneously, others claimed the lands to the west of Zuni Street. Opposed to Highland, they termed the section west of Denver proper the Highlands. On April 6, 1875, settlers and speculators incorporated the area stretching from West Colfax Avenue to West 38th Avenue between Zuni Street and Lowell Boulevard as the Town of Highlands. Potter Highlands was part of the new community.

By this time, much of the property had been repeatedly sold and replatted. Opposed to the general pattern of late 19th-century urban development where blocks are twice as long as they are wide, Potter Highlands has nearly square blocks. Besides allowing for the construction of residences on all four sides of the block, this provided space for an interior lot. That land was used for everything from grazing horses and cows to vegetable gardens to private parks. Into the 21st century, an amazingly wide variety of usages are found in the central squares of Potter Highlands.

The Humphrey family carved the land on which the Lumber Baron Inn is located, block two of Potter Highlands, into four large lots. On February 24, 1893, lots one, two, and four were completely redesigned as Blake's Resubdivision. It remembers Joseph A. and Anna S. Blake who had gotten the entire block on February 9, 1874. The Lumber Baron Inn occupies the western half of lot three.

There were scattered houses around Potter Highlands when the Town of Highlands emerged. For the most part, they were rather insubstantial farm shacks which soon disappeared. Others built for the ages. Such was the intention of Henri Foster at 2533 West 32nd Avenue. His residence is the oldest surviving structure in the district, dating from 1872–74. A key figure in forming the Town of Highlands, Foster was the community's inaugural clerk. Additionally, he dealt in real estate, brokered loans and mortgages, speculated in property, and was a banker. For some years, he had an office near West 30th Avenue and Zuni Street.

The Patrick H. McGowan House, 2633 West 37th Avenue, is a most distinctive dwelling half a block west of the Lumber Baron Inn. Around 1880, Hamilton Phillips designed it with an octagonal second floor on land McGowan had purchased in 1874. The owner was among the inaugural trustees of the Town of Highlands. Deeply interested in spiritualism, McGowan embraced the cult of octagon houses, a trend dating from the late 1840s. Houses with eight sides, proponents argued, provided more space per linear foot than did rectangular structures. More than that, they had better sunlight and ventilation, and provided for efficient and healthy living. The fad never caught on. Occupants found much of the odd-

The Patrick McGowan House at 2633 West 37th Avenue features an eight-sided second floor.

shaped spaces unusable. McGowan stayed in the house to about the time of World War I. He died in Oakland in December 1931. A subsequent owner discovered spiritualist magazines stashed away in the residence.

Almost every block in Potter Highlands has a similarly distinctive house. The area especially boomed in the 1880s. This was a decade when Denver exploded in population from 35,629 to 106,713 residents. Additionally, thousands more settled to the west of Zuni Street in the Town of Highlands, a community which expanded its borders west to Sheridan Boulevard in 1891. Six years earlier, on November 4, 1885, residents had officially incorporated it as the City of Highlands.

The suburb drew in affluent settlers who wanted to live beyond Denver proper. Some of their castles remain standing. Among them are the dwellings of James A. Fisher at 3224 Bryant Street, the Daniel Sayer–John Brodie House at 3631 Eliot Street, and the Henry Lee Manor at 2653 West 32nd Avenue. They and comparable houses were an eclectic blend of the popular styles of the day from Gothic to Victorian to Renaissance Revival.

Health considerations remained part of the allure of Potter Highlands. In the 1880s, with its unpaved streets, coal-fired furnaces, and many factories, Denver suffered severe air pollution. Those to the west of the city line at Zuni Street emphasized they were above all this, literally looking down on Denver as a blighted, sin-filled city. The City of Highlands, which prohibited alcohol, took steps to install water and sewer systems. It simultaneously worked to open schools and create parks while churches popped up.

The Masons focused on Potter Highlands. In 1890–91, Roger Woodbury, a foremost figure in the emergence of the Town of Highlands, took the lead in forming Highlands lodge #86 of the fraternal order. The society launched a building campaign in 1904, leading it to occupy its new temple at 3220 Federal Boulevard on September 15 of the next year. On October 30, 1928, with more than a thousand members and attracting the backing of other North Side branches, the Masons dedicated their second home three blocks to the north at 3550 Federal Boulevard. The Knights of Pythias acquired the old Masonic building, staying there until 1996 when the Delmonaco family purchased it, turning it into an events center/rental hall. The building was sold in 2013 when the new owner announced intentions to fill in the adjacent parking lots and possibly tear down the Potter Highlands landmark. Nearby, at the Gardens at St. Elizabeth, a seniors residence with a 14-story tower, was the Oakes Home, a tuberculosis sanitarium with ties to the Episcopalians. Numerous smaller facilities for convalescents were along West 33rd Avenue between Clay and Eliot streets.

The Panic of 1893 devastated Colorado. This was a traumatic Wall Street collapse. It severely hit Denver. Numerous banks failed amidst the implosion of the silver market. Not only did many formerly wealthy individuals lose their fortunes, but the City of Highlands verged on bankruptcy. Faced with overwhelming bonded indebtedness and a virtually empty treasury, it agreed to be annexed by the Mile High City in 1896 in exchange for Denver assuming the suburb's financial obligations.

As the Mile High City recovered from the recession, it primarily grew to the east of the newly opened Capitol. Already in the 1880s, Capitol Hill had emerged as the city's most prestigious section, complete with numerous castles. By the early 20th century, the elite increasingly settled in new palaces to the east and south of the Capitol and near the nascent Denver Country Club. Some Potter Highlands residents joined the trend, leaving North Denver for the East Side. Rather than a distinctive enclave of the wealthy, Potter Highlands, which still had numerous empty lots, became part of greater North Denver.

During the first 40 years of the 20th century, Potter Highlands slowly filled in. Generally, middle-class foursquares and bungalows proliferated along with some terraces and duplexes. After the return of peace in 1945, a new building boom saw the construction of ranch-style houses and many low-scale multi-family units. Some of the new structures replaced standing buildings. Others were on what had once been big yards. By this time, landlords had carved up many of the large 19th-century dwellings into apartments.

After World War II, Denver was seemingly embarrassed by its past. Boosters and real estate interests dismissed anything old as no good and obsolete. Frequently, the *Denver Post* heralded the destruction of a landmark for a faceless highrise as "good news today" on its front page. Compared to the devastation in the central business district and on Capitol Hill, the seemingly forgotten Potter Highlands managed to escape much of this "progress." Even so, there was a massive population shift during the 1950s and 1960s. Many who grew up in the area relocated to such northwest suburbs as Westminster, Wheat Ridge, Arvada, and

Photo by Phil Goodstein

*On September 15, 1905, the Masons consecrated their Highlands temple
at 3220 Federal Boulevard. It was subsequently the home of the Knights
of Pythias before becoming an events center/rental hall. John Mouat, the
builder of the Lumber Baron Inn, was a Mason.*

Lakewood. In their place, a large Hispano population moved in. Rents generally
were low while many landlords failed to keep their buildings in immaculate shape.

In the mid-1960s, many who were proud of Denver and its heritage, were sick
of the obliteration of the city's rich Victorian architecture. In March 1967, they
convinced the city to create the Denver Landmark Preservation Commission. This
was shortly after Dana Crawford saved the 1400 block of Larimer Street from the
Denver Urban Renewal Authority, transforming the space into the innovative and
highly profitable Larimer Square. On the heels of this, those who loved the city's
vintage buildings formed Historic Denver in 1970 to keep the Molly Brown House
standing. A wave of restoration saw a new appreciation of the city's pre–World
War I structures.

Among those embracing preservation were people who had grown up in sterile
suburbs. As they came of age in the 1970s, some discovered the intriguing edi-
fices, mature tree cover, and distinctive character of old houses and neighborhoods.
North Denver, long seen as the city's armpit, which was on the wrong side of the
river and the railroad tracks, started to become popular. Locals snapped up Ruth
Wiberg's pioneering 1976 history of the area, *Rediscovering Northwest Denver*—
she named John Mouat, the builder and first occupant of the Lumber Baron Inn,
"The Lumber Baron." Some who were unable to afford homes on Capitol Hill or
close to Washington Park moved to the North Side, heralding it as the city's most
authentic area and intriguing neighborhood.

Many new settlers, on acquiring rather dilapidated 19th-century houses, discovered that the restoration of their newly purchased property was a lot more expensive and difficult than they ever imagined. They found themselves putting endless sweat equity into their dwellings. Some gave up after a few years. Here and there, houses which had gone from being multi-family units back into single-family houses were again apartments. Simultaneously individuals who had long lived in the area moved to the suburbs, believing they were finally achieving the same middle-class success as had previous generations who exited for new neighborhoods after World War II.

To assure the integrity of the area's historic architecture, complete with its low-scale character, residents got the enclave near West 33rd Avenue and Bryant Street declared a Denver landmark district on April 20, 1979. They expanded the scope of the district to include most of Potter Highlands in an amended designation on February 25, 1987. Building owners in the district must receive permission from a review committee of the Denver Landmark Preservation Commission before remodeling the exterior of their structures to assure they maintain the character of the neighborhood's architecture. For some years, the Potter Highlands Preservation Association was a neighborhood group which sought to protect and promote the district. Activists have also supported Highland United Neighbors Incorpo-

Photo by Joseph Collier, Denver Public Library

In 1935, in the name of progress, the Marcus "Brick" Pomeroy Mansion, at the northeast corner of West 37th Avenue and Federal Boulevard, came down for a filling station. Even so, Potter Highlands mostly escaped the massive demolition of historic structures which swept much of central Denver in the mid-20th century.

Since the 1970s, dedicated homeowners and real estate investors have renovated numerous historic homes in Potter Highlands. Walter Keller, owner of the Lumber Baron Inn, oversaw the transformation of the pictured John Horne Chiles House at 2811 West 37th Avenue. He also was responsible for the refurbishment of such other properties in the district as 3659 Alcott Street, 3730–34 Bryant Street, and 2539 West 37th Avenue.

rated as an improvement association for the area south of West 38th Avenue to the east of Federal Boulevard.

Working with neighborhood activists, around 1987 the city installed some brick entryways to Potter Highlands at such intersections as West 38th Avenue and Bryant Street and West 35th Avenue and Zuni Street. The landmark protection has mostly worked in preserving the area from the massive glass and aluminum condo projects and McMansions which started to go up in parts of historic North Denver when the neighborhood again became most popular at the turn of the 21st century.

City landscaping efforts have also enhanced Potter Highlands. Especially noteworthy is the fate of Federal Boulevard. Initially, the street was simply known as The Boulevard, a grand parkway lined by elite houses. Over the years, the landscaping faded. In 1956, the administration destroyed most of the remnants of Federal Boulevard as a romantic parkway when it expanded the road into a four-lane arterial with an additional lane of parking. This came at the cost of chopping down many of the mature street trees.

Realizing the post–World War II generation had gone overboard in traffic "improvements," in 1997, with $2 million in federal funds, the city planted some trees along Federal Boulevard as part of a landscaping effort which saw the installation of narrow medians from West 20th Avenue to Interstate 70 in the name of restoring

The Woodbury Library, at the southwest corner of West 33rd Avenue and Federal Boulevard in Highland Park, is the literary center of Potter Highlands.

the road's grandeur. The administration also upgraded Highland Park, the spread on the west side of Federal Boulevard between West 32nd and West 33rd avenues. It is the home of the landmark neighborhood Woodbury Library. For years, the city has also talked about upgrading the streetscaping along West 38th Avenue, a prime commercial and residential strip.

Potter Highlands has remained a diverse area. Many of the post–World War II multiplex units continue as rentals. The population base ranges from individuals living in poverty to extremely affluent settlers. In some cases, Potter Highlands property owners have had their offices in their landmarks. The area is seemingly constantly changing while remaining the same. Part of a visit to the Lumber Baron Inn should be a stroll around the area, seeing how the district's largest and most active house fully complements the neighborhood. Within ten blocks of the bed and breakfast is virtually every style of domestic architecture which has been part of the Mile High City since the 1880s.

John Mouat

John Mouat was part of a large Scottish migration to Colorado in the 19th century. Born on July 28, 1848, he stemmed from Levenwick in the Shetland Islands, a bleak, treeless subarctic archipelago to the northeast of the Scottish mainland where the Atlantic Ocean meets the Norwegian Sea. His father, John Sr., lived from 1807 to 1894. His mother, Susanna, was born in 1807 and died in 1882.

In 1867, the young man set out to make his fortune in Liverpool. After a few years, he returned home before heading to Chicago in 1871. He was attracted to that city by labor contractors who eagerly sought men willing to work in the construction industry. Before long, he was a master carpenter, helping Chicago rebuild after its disastrous fire.

The lumber industry pulled Mouat to Colorado in 1873. As was the case with many other natives of Scotland, he was soon a lumber dealer and master contractor. Other Scottish entrepreneurs in Potter Highlands included Henry Lee at 2653 West 32nd Avenue, Daniel Sayer and John Brodie of 3631 Eliot Street, and Hugh MacKay at 3359 Alcott Street. Another Scot, William Bell, laid out the area south of West 32nd Avenue and west of Zuni Street as Scottish Village with such street names as Caithness Place, Argyle Place, and Firth Court.

The Mouat family was part of a wide-ranging Scottish clan. Members have spelled the name Mowat, Mowatt, Mouat, Mohat, Muot, Mouatt, and Movitt. An especially visible branch of the family has long dwelt in British Columbia. Some in the John Mouat family have pronounced the name "Mow-it"; others "Mow-out" or "Mow-at."

Construction was constant in soaring 19th-century Denver. After establishing Mouat Lumber Supply Company in 1878, the Shetlander incorporated the rapidly growing firm seven years later. In early 1891, the outfit became John Mouat Lumber & Investment.

In 1881, Mouat had returned to visit his family in the Shetland Islands. There he recruited a group of eager young men to join him in the Centennial State. Even-

Lumber Baron Inn

John Mouat was the lumber baron.

tually, about 20 to 30 Shetlanders had jobs among the 300 employees of Mouat Lumber. During a subsequent trip back to his native hearth, Mouat built a huge house for his parents. Levenwick eventually used it as the town hospital.

In addition to selling wholesale and retail building supplies, including blinds, doors, windows and stained glass, Mouat Lumber erected buildings across burgeoning Denver. Among John Mouat's projects was being general contractor of Moore School at the southeast corner of Ninth Avenue and Corona Street, a landmark which went up in 1889. He developed ties with its architect, Robert Roeschlaub, who designed some of the other buildings constructed by Mouat Lumber. All told, Mouat Lumber erected upwards of 200 structures. In the process, John Mouat worked with other leading architects such as William Quayle, John Huddart, Frederick Sterner, and George H. Williamson. The man who designed the Brown Palace, Frank Edbrooke, was responsible for the main Mouat administration building at the south corner of 26th and Blake streets.

The administrative offices of Mouat Lumber were initially located at 1625 16th Street (between Wazee and Wynkoop streets). He subsequently moved them to the Ernest & Cranmer Building at the south corner of 17th and Curtis streets. Workers constructed it in 1889 as the city's first structural-steel highrise.

Mouat Lumber expanded its operations through Colorado into Wyoming and New Mexico. It claimed to have the largest planing mill in the state. Members of the John Mouat family joined the business, including the firm's secretary, Jeremiah Mouat, and bookkeeper, Anthony Mouat. Malcolm Mouat was its manager.

For the most part, Mouat Lumber got along with labor. In March 1889, when the carpenters union announced it planned to strike the building industry on April 1 to assure the uniform eight-hour day, John Mouat stated that was not necessary. His company wanted to work with unionists. This was unlike some of the members of the Builders' and Contractors' Association who insisted nine hours must be the regular working day. Seeking to avoid a confrontation, Mouat stated his firm would go along with whatever agreement the union reached with other contractors.

In 1890, Mouat relocated his firm's building supply yards to near 26th and Blake streets where they covered 50 lots close to the railroad tracks, extending two blocks to 28th Street. He additionally had supply yards and holdings at the corner where Osage Street, Seventh Street, and West Colfax Avenue come together at the foot of the Colfax Viaduct. An additional Mouat business block was at 2150 Arapahoe Street.

Besides construction and selling supplies, Mouat focused on land speculation and development. A key effort was Swansea. This is the neighborhood east of York Street to the north of 40th Avenue. It emerged in 1873 as a separate community close to the railroad tracks where entrepreneurs launched the Swansea Smelting Works near the northeast corner of 45th Avenue and Columbine Street. They named it for a famous smelter in Wales which was the pioneer of a revolutionary smelting process. The Mile High smelter was short-lived. Poorly designed and managed, it quickly closed. Swansea School opened at the northeast corner of 46th Avenue and Columbine Street in 1891. Denver annexed the suburb, then part of Elyria, in May 1903.

In 1889–90, John Mouat acquired a good deal of the land of early Swansea, including the site of the abandoned smelter. He replatted the area from about 40th Avenue and York Street to near 48th Avenue and Thompson Court. Once the foreman for Mouat Lumber who became a company officer, Walter Thompson collaborated with him in the effort. Thompson was the namesake of Thompson Court, the 2650 east block which runs sporadically to the north of 43rd Avenue. It is parallel to Columbine Street, a road briefly known as Mouat Avenue.

For a while, Mouat Lumber had a supply yard between Columbine Street and Thompson Court near 46th Avenue while it built many houses in the area. An-

Photo by Phil Goodstein

In 1889, John Mouat was the general contractor of Corona School at the southeast corner of Ninth Avenue and Corona Street. On March 13, 1929, it became Dora Moore School, on the retirement of its longtime principal.

thony Mouat of 4577 Mouat Avenue and Isaac Mouat at 4709 Mouat Avenue, oversaw the company's interests in the area. Margaret Mouat, the wife of Anthony, remained at 4577 Mouat Avenue/Columbine Street into the 1920s.

John Mouat also focused on the North Side. His Mouat Lumber Company Re-Subdivision is the block bordered by West 24th and West 25th avenues and Grove and Hooker streets. He had about 60 adjacent lots and built many of the houses. Some have fixtures similar to those found in the Lumber Baron Inn. A number of Mouat Lumber employees lived in this section of North Denver.

The Mouat Lumber Company Re-Subdivision hinted at the lumber baron's political and economic idealism. He tried to run his firm as something of a cooperative. Besides family members, some of the officers had started as simple wageworkers. Among them were his fellow Shetlanders.

For a while, Mouat dwelt at 3 Fay Street, West 30th Avenue just to the west of Tejon Street. Besides his lumber firm, he was vice president of the North Side Building and Loan Company. He additionally focused on Aspen. During the 1880s, that town was Colorado's second silver city after Leadville. With R. F. Roberts, Mouat incorporated in Aspen in March 1885 as Mouat & Roberts. Part of Aspen's modern charm is the well-preserved core of some of the Victorian buildings Mouat & Roberts built. Mouat additionally had sawmills and lumbering operations in northern Park County.

Photo by Phil Goodstein

In the early 1890s, Mouat Lumber built houses along the west side of the 2400 block of Grove Street as part of a cooperative effort to house company employees. A couple of carpenters for the firm once dwelt at the pictured 2415 Grove Street.

Lumber Baron Inn

The 1890-vintage storage building of Mouat Lumber complex was at the north corner of 26th and Blake streets. Here were some of its employees. Around 1910–11, the structure came down for a paint factory.

The fortune of the Shetland native soared with the Denver and Aspen booms of the 1880s. On December 18, 1889, he paid $7,000 for lot three of block two of Potter Highlands, i.e., the southwest quarter of the block bordered by West 37th and West 38th avenues and Alcott and Bryant streets. Elizabeth Ashmed was the seller. She had procured the property on January 17, 1882, when she was Elizabeth Bailey prior to her marriage to Theodore Ashmed on June 6, 1883.

In 1890, Mouat constructed his palatial three-story, red-brick, sandstone-trimmed, 8,500-square foot home for himself, his wife Amelia, and five children: Margaret, John Jr., James Jeremiah, William, and Susan. It stands today as the Lumber Baron Inn.

To assure the house was a center of family life, his wife, a big woman, insisted on an extremely large kitchen. The residence was something of a showplace, using the latest, most fashionable, and best building supplies marketed by Mouat Lumber. Promoters celebrated the manor as "of the highest craftsmanship" in the region. It is the embodiment of Queen Anne architecture, a style of Victorian design especially popular in the 1890s which featured turrets, peaked roofs, and ornate woodwork.

Lumber Baron Inn

*Amelia Mouat, 1860–1936, was the wife of John Mouat and his part-
ner in overseeing their mansion at West 37th Avenue and Bryant Street.*

Lumber Baron Inn

*John Mouat was a deeply religious man. At times, such as in this letter to his
daughter, he tended to preach in his pronouncements.*

A coal-burning forced-air system, complemented by numerous coal-burning fireplaces, heated the home. To bring coal into the residence, there was a tunnel under the sidewalk along Bryant Street, connecting with a large basement coal bunker with stone walls. The chamber remains in place, an eerie remnant of 19th-century technology. It is adjacent to the room housing the furnace and laundry equipment. Excavations on the dirt floor of the tunnel have uncovered a broken shovel and some old clothes. A psychic exploring the area claimed there was a "room within a room," possibly the site of a burial from which the bones were later moved. The Lumber Baron Inn uses the basement for maintenance and service purposes. The 2,639-square-foot space has also been the owner's quarters as well as a place to stash the lodge's supplies.

Photo by Phil Goodstein

The woodwork of the first floor of the Mouat Mansion includes ornately designed rosettes.

The original address of the Mouat Mansion was 236 Euclid Avenue when Bryant Street was Third Street in Highlands. About the time Denver annexed Highlands in 1896, the city completely changed the street name and numbering system. It imposed an alphabet west of Zuni Street honoring great Americans. Bryant Street recalls poet and editor William Cullen Bryant.

Lumber Baron Inn

In 1885, John Mouat expanded his operations to Aspen.

To advertise his skills as a carpenter, lumber dealer, and contractor, Mouat designed the house with numerous varieties of fine hardwoods, including cherry, oak, poplar, sycamore, maple, and walnut. First-floor ceilings are 12 feet high. Ornately designed, hand-crafted rosettes decorate the 10-foot-high doorways.

A turret anchors the southwest corner of the house. This was a common theme in many mansions: builders and owners wanted some sort of a tower to emulate the castles of old. In places, the acoustics in the turret produce an echo. The turret features rounded glass, a new technology of the day. There is no sign a carriage house was ever built adjacent to the mansion.

The Panic of 1893 engulfed John Mouat. In addition to bankrupting many whose fortune was based on silver, it especially hit contractors and real estate investors such as Mouat. Borrowing heavily, he had built many properties on speculation, expecting to sell them for top dollar. Now he struggled to pay his bills while the value of his real estate collapsed. All the while, he retained a strong religiosity. At times, he preached more than answering questions in his personal correspondence.

In 1894 and 1895, the city filed tax claims on 2555 West 37th Avenue. Already on July 18, 1893, Mouat signed a quitclaim deed for the house over to John J. Riethmann, the president of German National Bank. The financial institution's receiver obtained the deed on October 22 of the next year. By this time, Riethmann was also suffering severe financial distress. He eventually went broke. In the early 20th century, the courts sold his estate, near First Avenue and University Boulevard, to the Denver Country Club as that organization's new home.

Photos by Joseph Collier

John and Amelia Mouat were the parents of five children. These show their daughters Susan, left, and Margaret.

Lumber Baron Inn
John Mouat is buried with his wife and close relatives in San Diego.

Mouat exited from his palace around 1897. For a while, the master builder dwelt on the west side of the 900 block of Federal Boulevard. It was area that had had great aspirations which never materialized. About 1902, he moved to 518 Pearl Street with his sons, Jeremiah and John Jr., before transferring to the adjacent 522 Pearl Street. The addresses were both part of stone-faced duplexes Mouat had built in the Alamo Placita neighborhood, an area he helped develop between Speer Boulevard, Sixth Avenue, and Downing Street. By the time Mouat relocated to Alamo Placita, he worked in real estate. Relatives Malcolm and William, who were involved in the mining industry, also shared 522 Pearl Street with him. All the members of the Mouat family listed their business address as suite 16 of 1643 Champa Street.

Near the end of the first decade of the 20th century, Mouat moved to San Diego. His last post before leaving the Mile High City was as the vice president of the Capital Security Company where his office was back in the Ernest & Cranmer Building. He stayed in San Diego until his death in 1934. Amelia passed away two years later. Members of his family remained in San Diego through the end of the 20th century, providing the Lumber Baron Inn with family photos.

In trying to hold on to Mouat Lumber, Mouat worked closely with the firm's vice president, William B. Palmer of 1721 Grant Street. Arriving in Denver shortly after the Civil War, Palmer had also long worked in the lumber business. Additionally, he had excellent political connections while he focused on real estate. In 1881, he was a county commissioner. Nine years later, Mouat Lumber was the

Around 1890, John Mouat teamed up with architect Frank Edbrooke to build the main administrative headquarters of Mouat Lumber at the south corner of 26th and Blake streets. In 1999, the structure emerged as the Blake Street Lumber Lofts. Its bricks match those on the Mouat Mansion.

contractor for Palmer's $14,000 mansion. Robert Roeschlaub designed it. The residence was right next door to the home of John J. Riethmann, the man who repossessed the Mouat Mansion. Palmer's manor has since been demolished. Mouat's partner passed away at age 68 in June 1911.

Palmer valiantly sought to help Mouat remain solvent. Around 1896, he oversaw a reorganization of the outfit as Mouat–Palmer Lumber, Palmer displacing Mouat as the company's president. Creditors endlessly hounded the business. On December 6, 1899, Judge Calvin P. Butler approved a creditors' plan for Hallack & Howard Lumber, another major contractor and building supply firm, to lease the shuttered Mouat yard at 26th and Blake streets for $100 a month. The agreement allowed Hallack & Howard to purchase the facility once the lease expired. That company so acquired the complex which had cost Mouat $300,000. McPhee & McGinnity, another major lumber and contracting firm, later occupied part of the property. William Scott Lee, who had served as mayor of Denver from 1885 to 1887, was the court-appointed receiver of Mouat Lumber. He oversaw the liquidation of the remnants of the Mouat empire at the tail end of the 19th century. In 1999, architects Tom Savory and Dale Reaves transformed the old Mouat headquarters at 2560 Blake Street into a 19-unit project, Blake Street Lumber Lofts.

The Fate of the Mouat Mansion

In the wake of the exit of John Mouat, his mansion repeatedly changed hands. Creditors sold the eastern half of lot three in 1897 for separate development. Thomas Feely acquired the land directly east of the Mouat Mansion four years later, soon selling two-thirds of it to Evelyn S. Read of 2720 West 37th Avenue. Her husband was carpenter Jason Read (1862–1940). He built 2539 and 2543 West 37th Avenue on the property, making the former address their home. His shop was at 2436 15th Street. After arriving in the Mile High City at age 23, he spent 46 years in the building field, retiring as a contractor in 1932. In 1904, he was the Prohibition Party candidate for sheriff of the new City and County of Denver. About that time, another house went up at 2533 West 37th Avenue on the eastern edge of lot three.

For a brief period, the Mouat Mansion was an apartment house. Between 1904 and 1909, the manor was the quarters of Denver Business University. This was a proprietary school teaching students bookkeeping, typing, filing, and similar skills. Elbert Mote ran it with owner Ellis J. Willits. It included dormitories on the premises, reaching out to North Denver residents who, it stated, could save on commuting costs by attending classes in the neighborhood. The school had the phone number 2452 Black.

Mote, who lived at 2925 Wyandot Street before moving to 4219 Vallejo Street, went to work as an instructor with Denver Public Schools after he sold Denver Business University to George H. Artlip in 1908. Formerly of Roanoke, Virginia, Artlip was an expert shorthand reporter who taught that craft. The "university," he advertised, was essentially a business high school where students learned trades which would get them white-collar jobs. It had both day and night classes. Shortly after Artlip announced a massive remodeling of the Mouat Mansion as part of an augmentation of Denver Business University, including an enhancement and expansion of the dormitories, he relocated the academy to 1742 Broadway where it soon faded from sight. The renovations never materialized.

COMPLIMENTS OF

The Denver Business University   Corner of W. 37th and Bryant

Lumber Baron Inn
Denver Business University occupied the Mouat Mansion from 1904 to 1909.

After Denver Business University exited, Hiram Grant Fowler acquired the house. Born in Hillsdale, Michigan, on June 15, 1863, he moved with his family to Blue Rappes, Kansas, as a boy. Within a few years, he emerged as a manufacturer of plaster of Paris. He arrived in Denver in 1903, serving as the secretary-treasurer of the Metals Tunnel Company, a mining venture.

It was among Fowler's many pursuits in seeking to acquire and market mineral wealth. Another of his other endeavors was the Honest John Mining and Milling and Tunnel Company. Additionally, he had considerable cattle holdings through his Laramie Live Stock Company. All his ventures listed 2555 West 37th Avenue as their business addresses, i.e., the Mouat Mansion. City and business directories describe Fowler as the secretary of the concerns. For a few years, he issued *Western Miner and Financier*. It was a tabloid-sized "weekly mining journal for investors and operators," printed on glossy paper. The publication faded away by the second decade of the 20th century.

Rumors endlessly floated that there might be more or a lot less to Fowler's enterprises than what appeared on the surface. His critics quoted Mark Twain's definition of a mine as "a hole in the ground owned by a liar." With the advent of the Securities and Exchange Commission and various efforts to regulate finance in the 1930s, Fowler encountered some turbulence with the government. He ostensibly retired in 1937. The 1940 census lists him as a laborer who did odd jobs.

On coming to Denver, Fowler took rooms at 1645 Welton Street. He soon made his home at 2456 West 38th Avenue. The 1912 city directory first places him at 2555 West 37th Avenue. He shared the house with his wife Laura Bradley. She was born about 1864. Some accounts make Iowa her birthplace; others put it in Kentucky. She was the mother of three children, Frank B., James H., and Anna Lee.

Almost from the time the Fowler family acquired 2555 West 37th Avenue, it rented space in it to other dwellers. Some were friends, acquaintances, or relatives. Many of the tenants were widows. Remodelings and modifications of the house were constant. The mansion was increasingly carved into more apartments.

Fowler was especially active in the Odd Fellows. He passed away at age 76 in mid-May 1940, dying from a heart attack at 2555 West 37th Avenue. Burial followed at Crown Hill Cemetery where his grave is unmarked. Soon after his demise, his wife passed away.

There was no ostensible family link between Hiram Fowler and Addison J. Fowler. The latter, born in Plymouth, Ohio, in 1860, came to Denver in 1886, about the same time he joined the bar. By the time of his death on February 23, 1937, he was a foremost attorney and community figure. Addison Fowler had had close connections with John Mouat who built the lawyer's house at 2401 Gaylord Street in 1890. That $9,000 residence, designed by architect Robert Roeschlaub, has many features and decorations comparable to the Lumber Baron Inn. It hints that Roeschlaub might have given Mouat a hand in crafting 2555 West 37th Avenue.

A. Lee Doud, Addison Fowler's longtime law partner, was a receiver of the Mouat Mansion, arranging the 1897 sale of the eastern half of lot three in a court-ordered tax sale. Doud also had an interest in the house at 2456 West 38th Avenue

2555 W. 37th Avenue, Denver, Colo., Home of Mr. and Mrs. H. G. Fowler and Friends, and THEIR Friends.

Lumber Baron Inn

This Lumber Baron Inn postcard features the Mouat Mansion during the early 20th century when longtime owner, Jim Fowler, grew up in the house.

where Hiram Fowler had once lived. The lawyer was most active in civic life, giving the dedication address for the City and County Building in 1932.

For a brief period, the daughter of Hiram and Laura Fowler, Anna Lee, took charge of the house. Born in Kansas around 1896, she had an eighth grade education. Early on, she married a German immigrant, Bruno Joseph Schlihs whose name has also been spelled Schlichs, and Schlips. Her children by him included Laura Jane (1917–22) and Robert Bruner Schlihs (1919–1988). The latter, for a while, lived, at the Mouat Mansion.

Anna Lee was subsequently the wife of Leigh B. Nelson of Chicago. Born on July 10, 1897, he died at age 35 on November 2, 1932, whereupon she came to Denver, joining her father's household. In 1927, Anna Lee had given birth to Gloria Nelson who was another part of the Hiram Fowler household. Gloria eventually moved backed to Chicago where she died in 1994. Martha L. Chittick, the sister of Hiram's wife, was also in the Mouat Mansion.

Frank Bradley Fowler, the brother of Anna Lee, was born in Kansas in 1891. A talented musician who once worked as a department manager for Denver Music Company of 1538–46 Stout Street, he also played in an orchestra. After his marriage to Hattie May Brown on August 15, 1922, he settled at 3241 West 22nd Avenue where he was a music teacher for Denver Public Schools. He rests next to his father at Crown Hill Cemetery.

In Denver, Anna Lee Fowler Nelson worked in the insurance industry. Shortly after her mother's death, she left the Mouat Mansion, moving to 3062 Albion Street.

Photo by Phil Goodstein

In 1890, John Mouat built 2401 Gaylord Street for Addison J. Fowler. While there was no ostensible link between him and Hiram Fowler, there were amazing connections between Addison Fowler and 2555 West 37th Avenue.

INDEPENDENT
CANDIDATES
for

Representatives to
General Assembly

City and County
of Denver

General Election
November 3, 1936

HENRY D.
BARRIE

Headquarters
2555 W. 37th Ave.
(OVER)

JAMES H.
FOWLER

We support both moral and legal rights of Labor—Human before property rights.

Lumber Baron Inn

In 1936, Jim Fowler, the longtime owner of 2555 West 37th Avenue, ran for the Colorado House of Representatives as an independent with the support of the Farmer–Labor Party and those advocating generous pensions for the elderly.

By 1950, she was back at 2555 West 37th Avenue, dying in the early 1960s. By this time, her other brother, James H. "Jim" Fowler, had long run the property.

Born in Blue Rappes, Kansas, on June 22, 1902, Jim Fowler grew up in Denver. Though living in the attendance district of North High, there is no record of him attending that school. On April 5, 1925, he wed the 18-year-old Lucille B. Martin in Littleton. They divorced on September 11, 1928. For a while, he was an insurance salesman for Prudential.

The Great Depression and the upheavals of the 1930s led Jim Fowler to reject his father's business emphasis. In light of the hard times, he argued that dispossessed citizens must stand up for themselves. To make this a reality, he threw himself into organizing the unemployed. Within a few years, he worked to build the Congress of Industrial Organizations (CIO), especially among farm workers, clerks, and meatpackers.

In 1936, Jim Fowler ran for the state legislature as an independent with the backing of the Townsend movement and the Farmer–Labor Party. The former advocated extremely generous pensions to senior citizens, far beyond what was paid by the nascent Social Security system. The latter had emerged after World War I out of the farmers' militant Non-Partisan League. It was something of a liberal reform alternative to both the Democrats and the Socialist and Communist parties. Fowler received 4,786 votes in November. At that time, all Denver candidates for the legislature ran at large. While his total was considerably more than the 883 ballots Communist Party leader William Dietrich received, and the 2,675 votes of the Farmer–Labor/Townsend candidate for Congress, it was nowhere close to the 89,704 ballots cast for the leading Democrat in the race or even the 50,000-plus votes gained by losing Republicans.

Fowler ran with a fellow resident of 2555 West 37th Avenue, Henry Daniel Barrie, who tallied 5,905 votes. Born in Sioux City, Iowa, on July 27, 1900, Barrie was a close and life-long friend of Fowler. Their mothers had had connections in

Iowa. During the 1930s, Barrie held a job with the Works Progress Administration. He was in and out of 2555 West 37th Avenue until virtually his death in September 1983.

The same year Fowler and Barrie sought places in the legislature, the Spanish Civil War broke out. Fowler supported the republican government against a virtual fascist coup of Francisco Franco backed by Hitler and Mussolini. To defend the Spanish Republic, in 1937 he enrolled in the Abraham Lincoln Battalion. This was part of the International Brigades, an effort of the Communist International to recruit volunteers to physically stop the fascists opposed to the policies of the United States, Britain, and France which more or less winked at fascist aggression in Spain. Approximately 2,800 other Americans joined Fowler in the International Brigades. The Spanish Republican government ordered the withdrawal of such soldiers in November 1938 in the desperate hope of reaching a negotiated agreement with Franco. This was a few months before the collapse of the Spanish Republic and the triumph of the fascists in March 1939.

Phil Goodstein collection

Before his death in 1981, Jim Fowler taught numerous classes at the Mouat Mansion through Denver Free University as part of his Center for Biological Self-Sufficiency.

Back in Colorado, Fowler worked as the manager of a vending machine company. Many viewed him as a Bolshevik. He was increasingly alienated from all parts of the financial system. Believing that capitalist agriculture was poisoning the food supply, he embraced organic gardening and called for a return to the land. For a while, he had a small farm in Idaho Springs—the climate there was not ideal for agriculture. By this time, Fowler stated he had been working in agriculture since he was a teenager.

Within a few years, Fowler returned to Denver, owning and occupying the Mouat Mansion. He carved it into upwards of 15 apartments. Some of the tenants were his comrades from Spain. During the McCarthy era in the 1950s, rabid anti-communists believed the house was a hive of Bolsheviks. The FBI spied on the building. The agency viewed anybody who had backed the International Brigades as a suspect, subversive character. Fowler and

Lumber Baron Inn

James "Pappy" Tatham was a close comrade of Jim Fowler who long lived in the basement of the Mouat Mansion. He oversaw its organic worm house. Here he stands by Lubin's Drugs at the northwest corner of West 38th Avenue and Clay Street in 1959.

associates, in turn, joked about their revolutionary ardor, nicknaming the Mouat Mansion "Smolny" in emulation of where Lenin had had the headquarters of the Bolsheviks during the 1917 Russian Revolution.

In cleaning out the mansion as he worked to renovate the house into the Lumber Baron Inn, Walter Keller discovered an English-language *Visitor's Guide to Leningrad* in the basement. Additionally, he came across some bullet shells there and even a few live bullets. In addition to them were some vintage, military-style wooden ammunition boxes. Perhaps Fowler and his comrades had been arming for the revolution.

Fowler increased his emphasis on the need for returning to the earth. He organized an organic food store. As part of his Center for Biological Self-Sufficiency, he plowed up much of the Mouat Mansion's huge yard as a garden and composting center. For a while, he identified himself as the secretary-treasurer of the Tri-County Organic Cooperative which had the business address of 2555 West 37th Avenue. He additionally helped form and oversee the Colorado Organic Growers and Marketers Association—he had been working in consumer cooperatives since the end of World War II. Collaborating with the Sierra Club, he was a pioneer in pushing household recycling. The Center for Biological Self-Sufficiency had a four-acre demonstration plot near the old Stapleton Airport at 54th Avenue and Rosyln Street.

Working with a close cohort, James Tatham, known by one and all as Pappy Tatham, Fowler further dug up the stretch between the sidewalks and the street for his garden. A favorite plant was comfrey that had numerous medicinal uses. Besides the garden, the backyard included a 15-foot by 20-foot concrete slab for parking. Most of all, the yard featured an "organic worm house." "Earth Worms" was painted on the Bryant Street wall of the outbuilding that Fowler and Tatham used as a composting center. (While emphasizing the organic garden, Fowler neglected most of the trees on the estate. Few were still standing by the time of his death.)

During the 1960s and 1970s, Fowler steadily emphasized community gardening. To help instruct people how to make it a reality, he was among those who embraced Denver Free University. This was an adult education program that emerged in 1969 as an alternative to the sterility of colleges. Beginning in 1973, Fowler taught organic gardening classes at the Mouat Mansion through the school. Simultaneously, he urged locals to dig up vacant lots and use them as their urban farms. The demand for such plots became so popular that city hall embraced the

Lumber Baron Inn

Emphasizing gardening, Jim Fowler had an organic worm house in the backyard of the Mouat Mansion. Here it is in the background in 1959 when a neighboring boy took a picture of his new go-cart.

The Mouat Mansion lost its front porch when Jim Fowler ran it as a low-income apartment house. This is what it looked like in the 1970s.

effort in 1974, opening some city-owned vacant lots to senior citizens as community gardens. This program eventually grew into Denver Urban Gardens, an effort which mostly consisted of elite, locked-off gardens by the 21st century. It was necessary to fence off the gardens, some advocates explained, to keep people from stealing the produce. In other places, backers of community gardens advertised that they used their excess produce to help feed the homeless.

Fowler was still active as a gardener and teacher at the time of his unexpected death in November 1981. His passing was so sudden, apparently the result of a fall, that the daughter of a woman to whom Jim Fowler had been briefly married in the early 1970s, suspected foul play in his demise. No investigation was ever made into the exact nature of his death.

The Mouat Mansion was in extremely dilapidated shape by the time of Fowler's passing. He had always cared far more about providing lodging for low-income individuals than preserving the luxury of yesterday's ruling class. This was in keeping with his 1936 campaign slogan of "Human before Property Rights."

During Fowler's tenure, workers ripped away original fixtures and destroyed much of the mansion's surviving charm. Increasingly, it was a flophouse. Evidence on the exact number of units and the nature of who and how many people lived in the residence during the 1950s, 1960s, and 1970s is quite nebulous. Tenants were often highly transient and did not always show up in city directories and census counts.

Walter Keller Takes Charge

Walter Charles Keller is the modern Lumber Baron, the owner of the inn whose dedication and vision have made it possible. Born in 1969, he came to Denver as an infant, right about the time his parents bought the house at 2338 Federal Boulevard. Mass foliage guarded that dwelling from the traffic along the arterial. The domicile dates from the day when a location along Federal Boulevard was a premier residential address.

The great-grandfather of Walter Keller, the owner of the Lumber Baron Inn, ran a candy store in St. Joseph, Missouri, at the turn of the 20th century.

Franklin E. Keller Jr., Walter's father, was from St. Joseph, Missouri. The modern Lumber Baron's great-grandfather on his father's side was his namesake, Walter Charles "Pop" Kennedy, the operator of a leading St. Joseph hardware store. Walter retained close St. Joseph connections into the second decade of the 21st century. Among them was running the Shakespeare Chateau, a luxury bed and breakfast in that Missouri River community best known as the eastern terminus of the Pony Express.

The Denver Lumber Baron operates the Shakespeare Chateau with Isobel McGowan. For some years she owned the house at 3600 Clay Street, a couple of blocks away from the Mouat Mansion. Now and then, she performed in murder mysteries at the Lumber Baron Inn. The Shakespeare Chateau, a renovated Victorian manor, is among the many spinoffs from the Lumber Baron Inn. Keller reopened

Lumber Baron Inn

On leaving high school in 1941, Franklin E. Keller joined the Army Air Forces. Until his death in 1998, he was always extremely proud of his service during World War II. He was the father of the owner of the Lumber Baron Inn.

the bed and breakfast in the early 21st century after it had been shuttered for about a decade.

Keller's father was born on September 3, 1923, in St. Joseph. After graduating from high school in 1941, he married his high school sweetheart, Leda Jean Ziemendorf. Soon after the wedding, Franklin Keller hitchhiked to California to join the military. Assigned to the Army Air Forces, he was part of the acclaimed Red Devils 96th Bombing Squadron during World War II. The Distinguished Flying Cross was among his decorations. He left the service on the return of peace as a sergeant.

Back in St. Joseph, Keller was the father of four children, Kathy, Kerry, Kristy, and Franklin III. He worked in a number of jobs, including the division of industrial inspection of the state of Missouri. The veteran frequently showed up at civic occasions while being politically involved in St. Joseph. His state inspector position and civil activism gained him the honorary southern title of "Colonel Keller." Many simply referred to him as "The Colonel."

In 1965, Franklin Keller abandoned his family, leading to his divorce from Leda Jean. Soon thereafter, he married Mary Ann Boeck of St. Paul in Washington, D.C., agreeing to adopt her young son Christopher. Back in St. Paul, Mary Ann gave birth to Walter. When he was six months old, the family moved to Denver in early 1970.

For some years, Franklin Keller had worked as a traveling salesman for Nord Engineering. It manufactured special photo equipment, primarily for studios. Wishing to expand its operations in the American southwest, it assigned Keller to oversee its sales there. Having the choice of headquarters in Albuquerque, Colorado Springs, or Denver, he chose the Mile High City.

Keller always drove around in the latest Cadillac. Besides handling sales for Nord Engineering, he dabbled in numerous other fields. Most of all, he scoured flea markets and garage sales, accumulating a wide array of unusual possessions. Eventually, he set up shop in the extremely large carriage house of 2338 Federal Boulevard. It served as the quarters of his Keller Engineering, a firm dealing in automobile parts, especially tires, air compressors, and tools. Additionally, the elder Keller was intensely involved with the Democratic Party, being a most visible regular at the North Denver party's Saturday morning sessions at Ernie's, a bar/restaurant near West 44th Avenue and Eliot Street. For a while, he was a district captain. In his later years, the Colonel was a frequent volunteer at the Veterans Administration Medical Center.

Mary Ann Boeck Keller passed away in 1989. Franklin Keller died at age 75 on September 16, 1998, after a 17-month fight with throat and lung cancer. The funeral was held at Our Merciful Savior Episcopal at West 32nd Avenue and Wyandot Street. As a highly decorated airman, Franklin Keller's ashes were placed in Arlington National Cemetery.

After going to Denver Public Schools during the busing era, including Boulevard School directly across the street from his home and Lake Middle School at West 18th Avenue and Lowell Boulevard, Walter Keller stood out during his four years at North High School. He was head boy during his senior year in 1986–87. Additionally, he was class salutatorian and the captain of the soccer team. Under him, the student body adopted a new North logo.

While at North, Walter experienced turbulence at home. His parents divorced while his mother suffered from bouts of mental illness. This led him to be "emancipated" from his parents in September 1986 when he was declared a ward of the Juvenile Court. It oversaw his adoption that month by Lino P. and Christina Gonzales. His adoptive father was then principal at North. As a star high school student, Keller won a full four-year scholarship from the Masons to attend Colorado College in Colorado Springs.

In 1874, the Congregationalists opened Colorado College, the territory's first true four-year college. Besides being part of a missionary outreach effort to provide enlightenment for the Rocky Mountains, it was for students suffering from tuberculosis. Styling itself the Yale of the West, Colorado College established a reputation as an excellent small, liberal arts school.

There Walter met Maureen Coll. Born in 1968, she had grown up in San Francisco. On graduating from high school she headed to the Colorado Springs academy, earning her bachelor's in 1990, followed by receiving a master's in education the next year.

Like Walter, Maureen was interested in the Colorado College student government. They ran for it on the same slate. Though they both lost, they developed

Lumber Baron Inn

As a toddler, Walter Keller had long hair. Here he is with his brother Christopher and his parents, Franklin and Mary Ann, around 1972.

binding ties. She was very much an entrepreneur. Since age 14, she had regularly worked in the food and hospitality industries, including frequently spending summers at her family's small commercial apple farm in upstate New York. Maureen had additionally worked as a newspaper carrier and had briefly helped run a delicatessen in Seattle. At quite a young age, she emerged as the headwaiter at a small San Francisco restaurant.

In college, both desired to become educators, earning teaching certificates. On Walter's graduation in 1991, they decided to live together in Denver. They took jobs with Denver Public Schools. During his first year in 1991–92, he oversaw the gifted and talented program at Kepner Middle School. For his efforts, he won the inaugural Sallie Mae Teacher Award in Denver, a $1,000 grant from a federally backed agency insuring student loans which went to the best first-year teacher in the district. The number-two contender was Maureen who, after a year teaching in Colorado Springs, had been a seventh-grade instructor at Cole Middle School.

Walter returned to North High for the 1992–93 schoolyear where he was the director of student activities while teaching American government/social studies. Additionally, he served as the North representative to the board of the Denver Classroom Teachers Association. This is the Denver chapter of the Colorado Education Association, the union representing instructors.

Besides education, Walter and Maureen embraced Denver history and traditions. They were greatly attracted to the city's surviving 19th-century buildings. This was when historic preservation was a rising tide. After the continued destruction of many architecturally stunning buildings, activists convinced the city to increase the scope and powers of the Denver Landmark Preservation Commission. Residents joined the campaign to create large landmark districts.

A push for beds and breakfasts was part of the trend. In March 1987, Chuck Hillestad opened the city's first modern bed and breakfast, the Queen Anne Inn, in the Frank Pierce House at 2147 Tremont Place, a residence which had been badly trashed out and long neglected. A couple of years later, Jim and Diane Peiker did a comparable renovation in transforming the stone Wilbur S. Raymond House at 1572 Race Street into the internationally acclaimed Castle Marne.

After opening the lodge, the Peikers taught a class about their experiences through Colorado Free University. Among those taking it were Walter and Maureen. They hoped to create an equally impressive place, one highlighting the historic charm of North Denver.

Strolling about the North Side and looking at large, vintage houses, Walter and Maureen discovered the Mouat Mansion. They believed it was the ideal location for a different kind of bed and breakfast. With its huge lot and a third-floor ballroom, they viewed the property as the site of weddings and group functions. Other inns lacked the space to host large gatherings.

The house was boarded up and bank owned when the couple first espied it. David G. Copp of Westminster had acquired the residence on June 19, 1982, from Jackie H. Fowler. The latter, the niece of Jim Fowler, had inherited it. At the time of his death she was the office manager of Scott–Thornton Orthopedics, a firm at

Photo by Phil Goodstein

The Castle Marne, a bed and breakfast, occupies the Wilbur Raymond Mansion at 1572 Race Street. After taking a class there on how to operate a bed and breakfast, Walter and Maureen Keller renovated the Mouat Mansion into the Lumber Baron Inn.

724 17th Avenue selling wheelchairs, walkers, and comparable supplies to individuals having mobility and health problems. She briefly lived in the Mouat Mansion in 1981–82.

Rudy Schware was the attorney for the Jim Fowler estate. Born in New York in 1914 of a poor immigrant family, he joined the youth group of the Communist Party in 1932. Two years later, he relocated to California where he was active in the labor movement. During the Spanish Civil War, he recruited volunteers for the Abraham Lincoln Battalion.

Schware left the Communist Party in 1940 in the wake of the Hitler–Stalin Pact. He settled in New Mexico after military service as a paratrooper in the South Pacific during World War II. On graduating from the University of New Mexico, he entered its law school, disclosing his communist past to the dean. When he graduated, the New Mexico Board of Bar Examiners blocked Schware from taking the bar examination. It ruled that his prior communist affiliation meant he lacked the appropriate good character to become an

Lumber Baron Inn

Maureen Coll, Walter's first wife, was his partner in renovating the Mouat Mansion into the Lumber Baron Inn. She measures the space by the graffiti-besmirched wall in the back parlor from which the mantel had been stolen.

attorney. In a landmark case, in 1957 the United States Supreme Court ordered his right to take the bar examination. Three years later, Schware settled in Denver, being involved in numerous progressive causes while defending clients in politically charged cases. He managed to save pieces of the beveled diamond glass from the Mouat Mansion, handing them down to the Lumber Baron Inn. Schware arranged for some of Jim Fowler's books, especially his collection on agriculture, to go to the University of Colorado. Supposedly, the Communist Party received a valuable Fowler stamp collection.

On obtaining the Mouat Mansion, Copp announced plans to renovate it. Despite this, he expanded the manor to about 23 units. Many of the apartments were in worse shape than they had been before he gained possession of the house. Residents of some of the units shared baths. Financial problems, compounded by the economic crisis of the late 1980s, led him to quit work on the effort.

On March 16, 1990, a city inspector sent Copp a six-page letter outlining some of the many code violations at the Mouat Mansion. Vegetation was growing in the foundations of the house. Gutters and downspouts were disconnected. Weeds were omnipresent. Loose wires dangled from the walls. Besides many broken windows, there were numerous gaps between the windows and the walls. In addition to ordering Copp to correct the problems within 30 days, the missive stated

Lumber Baron Inn

The Mouat Mansion when Walter Keller purchased it on April Fools Day 1991.

that more improvements might be required upon a further, more extensive examination of the property. Rather than heeding the order, Copp walked away from the
house, allowing it to go into foreclosure. Some accounts describe it as having
been a crack house. Tales circulated that a gangbanger who had lived there had
had his leg chopped off in an ax fight at the residence.

World Savings repossessed the house from Copp. Its appraisers stated the mansion was worth $265,000. Unable to find a purchaser at that price in a depressed
real estate market, the thrift urged interested buyers to make an offer. It agreed to
sell it to the Kellers for $80,000, carrying the mortgage. They put down half that
amount.

The mortgage date was April 1, 1991. It was ominous that they had purchased
it on April Fools Day. Or so members of their families and real estate advisers
informed them, viewing the boarded-up house with its huge, unkempt lot as an
albatross. At the time of the purchase, Maureen was 22 years old; Walter was 21.
Both quickly realized that they had not known exactly what they were getting into.
Even so, they believed they had gotten an excellent deal. To affirm their commitment, they wed shortly after obtaining the property.

Creating the Lumber Baron Inn

Placing all their assets into the Mouat Mansion, the Kellers continued to teach school while settling in the large, rambling, dilapidated house. The plumbing had frozen. The wiring system was ancient and below code. Nor did the heating system work. For a year and a half they lived in the dining room, the only place in which they could arrange dependable heat. Their three Dalmatians shared the space and protected the house.

Before long, the two were spending virtually all of their spare time fixing up the mansion. To do a better job of it, Walter apprenticed to Dave Cole. A veteran carpenter and contractor who was most knowledgeable about Denver's past and deeply committed to historic preservation, Cole explained the possibilities and problems of renovating the Mouat Mansion while Walter gained a greater appreciation of the task that was before him.

Maureen soon gave up on teaching to devote her efforts to making the inn a reality. She was the president of the Lumber Baron Inn, their personal firm. Much of their initial effort was pure elbow grease, including removing graffiti and supposed blood stains from the floors. They had to spend $15,000 to haul debris from the residence. This included trucking out 14 bathrooms and kitchens as the prelude to replumbing the building.

Among other problems, the mansion had been looted. As home restoration became most popular, unethical antique dealers and scroungers often broke into abandoned Victorian structures, making off with the fixtures. The Kellers counted eight hand-crafted fireplace mantels as missing, structures of cherry, oak, walnut, and sycamore. Some stained-glass windows had also disappeared as had a number of heavy, hardwood doors. Evidence showed that someone had unsuccessfully sought to make off with the ornately carved oak newel on the main staircase.

After continually scouring for funds in the hope of making the Mouat Mansion into a special inn, Walter and Maureen obtained a $300,000 loan from Eagle Bank in Broomfield. To get it, they drew on personal and political connections and

Lumber Baron Inn

Walter Keller played a hands-on role in the transformation of the trashed-out Mouat Mansion into the Lumber Baron Inn.

received a guarantee from the Small Business Administration. By the time they secured the money, the Kellers estimated they had invested $20,000 into the house in addition to $50,000 in sweat equity.

With the bank loan in hand, having gotten the backing of the West 38th Avenue Merchants Association, the Lumber Baron Inn received an additional $300,000 loan from the Mayor's Office of Economic Development. The Historic Fund of the Colorado Historical Society, which draws its money from gambling revenues, awarded the Kellers $100,000. Additionally, they obtained $100,000 in tax credits. They used some of the funds to pay off the $40,000 balance of their mortgage to World Savings.

To make the renovation a reality, they applied for planned unit development (PUD) zoning in 1992 from the existing R-2 classification of the property. The PUD allowed them to include the bed and breakfast and the hosting of events. Ordinance 430 of 1992 granted the PUD. It specified the inn was to have no more than five guest rooms. To get city council to adopt the measure, the Kellers worked closely with the neighborhood, explaining their project to those living nearby. The same was true in obtaining a liquor license so they could serve and sell alcohol at events.

More than 70 percent of the bulk of the property, they promised, would be landscaped as open space. The building itself occupied 3,302 square feet of the lot. Another 4 percent of the 14,000 square-foot spread consisted of a driveway/small parking area.

David C. Anderson, of Andrews and Anderson of Golden, was the architect overseeing the restoration. Working closely with the Kellers, he faced a severe challenge in figuring out the exact layout of the original house—none of John Mouat's plans for the house survive. Nor are the building permits of the City of Highlands intact. Consequently, the renovators had to make educated guesses about the exact floor plans and the way Mouat had built the house.

Roberts Construction, a firm owned by former city councilman/manager of public works Bill Roberts, was general contractor. When signing on, Roberts promised his firm would complete the job for a guaranteed price within 90 days. Despite this, the effort took a year, coming in far over budget. Roberts received much of the disputed amount in a subsequent mandatory arbitration. The cost overrun diluted all of the Lumber Baron Inn's reserves and forced the Kellers to increase their loan from Eagle Bank.

Here and there, parts of the interior restoration look unfinished. In places, the wood is blemished and some of the fixtures are missing. This is deliberate. On the advice of experts at the National Trust for Historic Preservation, the Kellers decided to keep a few building scars in place to show visitors where hallways had been. A careful look also reveals some of the extreme remodeling which had blemished the original integrity of the mansion. The Lumber Baron Inn additionally left a few spots bare to illustrate how many of the original decorations of the house had disappeared.

Old houses require constant upkeep. This is especially the case with a historic mansion. Work on maintaining the building and enhancing its original integrity is seemingly endless. Long-pondered and delayed projects have included restoring the widow's walks. Adding an elevator has been stymied by funding problems and the arcane world of historic tax credits. Especially on the second floor, the Lumber Baron Inn features pictures of the Mouat Mansion before and during the renovation.

As the project was underway, the Kellers received highly favorable media attention. After devoting three and a half years to the effort, they opened the Lumber Baron Inn in September 1994. It immediately received great ac-

Lumber Baron Inn

Renovation of the Mouat Mansion required almost the complete reconstruction of parts of the house. Here work is underway in converting the second-floor master bedroom into the Honeymoon Suite.

claim, reaping many awards. Among them was being "A Great American House" from the National Trust for Historic Preservation. The facility reached out to the community, offering Sunday brunches, Murder Mystery Dinners, and Christmas craft shows. The inn holds a weekly open house so the curious can come in and discover it as a marvelous neighborhood resource and an ideal place to stay on special occasions. It has been part of numerous house tours, usually cosponsoring them. Among them has been an annual Jewels of Highlands, an event where about 10 homeowners open their residences to those appreciating distinctive dwellings. Proceeds from it go to benefit a local school.

Most of all, the Lumber Baron Inn has been a romantic place for marriages. Besides having facilities for extraordinary ceremonies, it has a large garden and ballroom for receptions. Newspapers and magazines have celebrated it as the place for the most memorable romantic night in the city. Many Lumber Baron Inn guests are locals who check in for mini-vacations and weekend getaways, including those wishing a special night to celebrate anniversaries.

The back yard features statuettes and a small gazebo. During the summer, it is the gathering spot for murder mysteries and the site of weddings and receptions. At times, the facility advertises itself as the Lumber Baron Inn and Gardens.

John Daniel Kennedy Keller has been part of various activities at the Lumber Baron Inn. Maureen gave birth to him on August 28, 1997. The seven-pound,

Lumber Baron Inn

The Lumber Baron Inn shortly after it opened in September 1994.

John Keller, born on August 28, 1997, has grown up at the Lumber Baron Inn. Here he helps his father during a wedding reception in 2005.

three-ounce infant was named John Daniel for her father and Kennedy for the Kennedy branch of the Keller family. Maureen especially sought to assure her son received a top-notch public school education.

With money in hand from a 1998 bond issue, Denver Public Schools (DPS) promised a new school for the neighborhood. The Kellers were second to none in seeing that the district acquired the vacant Catholic Mount Carmel High School at West 37th Avenue and Zuni Street, two blocks east of the Lumber Baron Inn. Though they valiantly sought to save the structure, which dated from the late 1940s and had been designed by acclaimed architect Temple Buell, DPS insisted on demolishing the landmark for a new educational building.

The area's school board representative, Rita Montero, called for making what became Ana Marie Sandoval School into a fundamental academy, a place emphasizing the basics with strict drilling and old-fashioned discipline. In opposition, Maureen and Walter crusaded to operate it as a dual-language Montessori program, taking in students from three years of age in preschool through fifth grade. After a long fight, including the defeat of Montero in her 1999 bid for re-election, DPS committed itself to the Montessori program. Sandoval School opened in August 2001.

By the time John Keller enrolled at Sandoval School, differences had separated Walter and Maureen. After disposing of the adjacent 2543 West 37th Avenue, a house they had acquired as possibly their home, she talked about selling of the inn in the hope of having a more traditional family life. When Walter balked, she

On April Fools Day 2006, Walter Keller (Batman) wed Julie Hardesty (Catwoman) at the Lumber Baron Inn in a Masquerade at the Mouat Mansion. During the ceremony, they posed on the grand staircase of the inn with Walter's son John, the boy scientist.

observed that maybe it was time for them to part. Consequently, the marriage collapsed in 1999. By the time they separated she was a Realtor. He kept the Lumber Baron Inn.

On April 1, 2006, the 15th anniversary of his purchase of the Mouat Mansion, Walter wed Julie Hardesty. She grew up in Cheyenne, being a star swimmer at that city's East High School. After attending the University of Wyoming, she made her way through the Western Culinary Institute in Portland, Oregon, graduating with honors. The chef moved to Denver after having worked in the food service industry in Louisiana and Wyoming.

Julie met Walter at a Murder Mystery Dinner at the Lumber Baron when he was tending bar. She gave him a dollar tip with her phone number scribbled on the bill. Before long, she was his partner as innkeeper. She joined him in writing the scripts of murder mysteries, sometimes performing in them. Julie handles the extensive food operations of the Lumber Baron Inn, including cooking its banquets. The *North Denver Tribune* featured the story of the dollar bill when announcing Walter's marriage to Julie.

Their wedding was a grand double event. Besides the traditional ceremony, it was a memorable Masquerade at the Mouat Mansion where members of the audience were expected to show up in the appropriate costumes. Staged as a play, it featured Batman (Walter) wedding Catwoman (Julie). John was the boy scientist in the performance.

For a while, Julie offered guests a specially prepared five-course, room-service candlelight dinner. They ordered it before they checked in, going through the menu with Julie. Though the feast was extremely popular, it strained her ability to get up early the next morning to prepare breakfast. She categorically refused to allow Walter to prepare breakfast even though he had done so while running the Lumber Baron Inn before their marriage. Since the Lumber Baron Inn is foremost a bed and breakfast, she reluctantly had to put aside the candlelight dinners. Walter and Julie have pondered some means of reinstating them as a special feature.

Julie's recipes are not secret. She is ready to share them with the curious. Such is the case with her acclaimed Stuffed French Toast Crème Caramel, serving two:

1. Liberally coat medium soufflé cups with pan spray.

2. In a mixing bowl combine 3 large eggs, 1/2 cup of half & half, 1 teaspoon vanilla extract. Whip until frothy.

3. Cube 3 slices of French bread from a loaf (one-inch thick) and 1 cinnamon raisin bagel.

Lumber Baron Inn

Weddings, mystery evenings, and period fireplace mantels are among the features of the Lumber Baron Inn. Walter Keller primps himself here as Kamilla Rugburn for her wedding in a drama connecting all three themes.

Photo by Phil Goodstein

Besides overseeing the kitchen at the Lumber Baron
Inn, Julie Keller helps write, produce, and act in mur-
der mysteries. In this scene, she pies Walter.

4. Mix bread/bagel into batter until well coated and place in refrigerator overnight.

5. The next morning, preheat oven to 400 degrees.

6. Bake soufflés at 400 degrees for 30 minutes.

7. While baking, prepare caramel sauce: In a heavy sauce pot combine 1 stick
of butter, 1/4 cup of brown sugar, 3 tablespoons maple syrup, and 1 teaspoon of
vanilla. Bring to a boil. Let simmer for 10 minutes then add 1 tablespoon heavy
whipping cream. Return to simmer until soufflés are out of oven.

8. At the 30-minute mark, test with a toothpick inserted into the center of the
soufflé. If it comes out clean, it is done.

9. Remove from soufflé cup onto a surface and turn upside down. Insert a
knife into the bottom of the soufflé in order to stuff 1 tablespoon of cream cheese
into it.

10. Place stuffed soufflé on a plate and top with sauce.

11. Options are to top with pecans or other whole nuts. In the fall, it is nice to
use fanned slices of a green apple.

Lumber Baron Politics

After leaving his teaching post at North High School to work fulltime at the Lumber Baron Inn, Walter Keller kept his ties with his alma mater. For a few years, he served as the community member of its collaborative decision-making board. In the early 21st century, he went against the grain of most North supporters. At that time, he opposed spending approximately $34.5 million for a thorough rehabilitation of the original 1911 wing of the school. He believed North High was beyond repair, both physically and in terms of its academic reputation. What the North Side needed, he boldly asserted, was a new building for a Highlands High School. Such an effort, he predicted, would give the academy and neighborhood a fresh identity. Many of his fellow alumni loudly scorned his views. In 2011, dignitaries dedicated the restored school building on its centennial. Soon thereafter, Denver Public Schools gave half of the structure over to a charter school.

Despite sometimes taking such unpopular stances, Keller had strong political ambitions. No sooner had the Lumber Baron Inn opened than it was the site of fundraisers and events for Democratic politicians ranging from Dennis Gallagher to Susan Barnes-Gelt to Lee White to John Hickenlooper. In 2003, Keller was an early sponsor and supporter of the last's mayoral campaign. After Hickenlooper won city hall that June, the mayor-elect's transition team met at the Lumber Baron Inn to prepare the new administration.

Already in college, Walter had strong interests in politics. Dabbling as an artist, he drew numerous political cartoons. Among them was a graphic used by those pushing through legalized gambling in Cripple Creek, Black Hawk, and Central City in 1990. Eight years later, having opened the Lumber Baron Inn, Walter was a North Denver leader of a successful bond improvement issue heavily advocated by Mayor Wellington Webb. Building on this, Keller stated he was ready to run for a council-at-large seat in the 1999 city elections. At the last minute, under the pressure of leaders of the Democratic Party, he pulled out of the race. This was

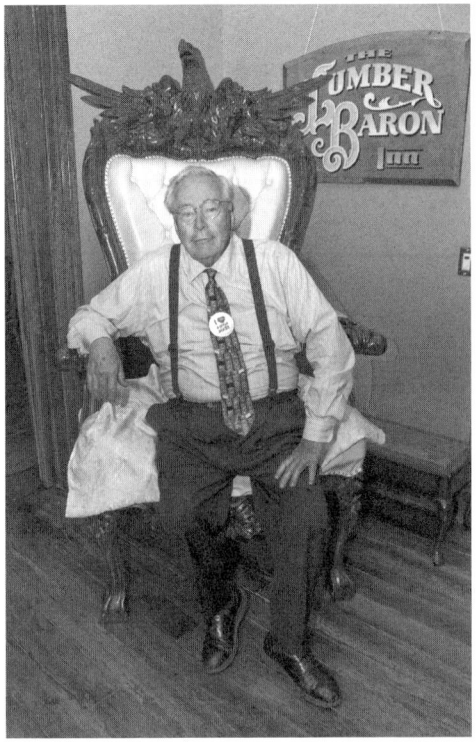

Photo by Tom Torgove

Politicians have held many events at the Lumber Baron Inn. Here lifelong North Denver resident Dennis Gallagher, who has held some elective office or another since 1970, sits in the throne in the front parlor of the mansion. His pin states, "I love a good audit," referring to his post as city auditor which he won in 2003. An associate of Walter Keller's father, Gallagher was an early and ardent supporter of renovating the Mouat Mansion into the Lumber Baron Inn.

about the time he was suffering marital problems.

In 2002, Keller launched a bid for an open seat for district five of the Colorado House of Representatives. The constituency ranged from North Denver to Globeville to western Capitol Hill, including most of downtown. Calling himself a "young entrepreneur," he set out to walk the district, meeting people and discussing the issues of the day.

The Democratic establishment seemingly rallied to Keller's cause. He easily won the caucuses against two opponents. Though in recent years the district had been something of a Hispanic seat, no Latino sought the post. At the most, Joel Judd of 2904 West 24th Avenue petitioned his way onto the primary ballot. Born in Denver in 1951, he graduated from George Washington High School in southeast Denver. The family of Judd's uncle had large and old real estate holdings, including in lower downtown. In a stunning upset, Judd swept the primary by a two-to-one margin, going on to win the seat in November where he served for eight years. Term limited in 2010, Judd failed in a bid for a place in the state Senate. Lucia Guzman defeated him, the same woman whom the Kellers had backed in 1999 against Rita Montero for the school board.

In some ways, the defeat in his political bid was a blessing in disguise for Keller. It gave him more independence, allowing him to speak out on controversial issues while focusing more on the Lumber Baron Inn. He often served as master of ceremonies at the gatherings of politicians at the Mouat Mansion whereby he seemingly knew everybody. A variety of neighborhood groups continued to meet at the Lumber Baron Inn while politicians haunted the premises.

Ghostly Guests

While living in the dilapidated mansion, Walter felt that something or somebody could have been sharing the dwelling with him, his wife, and his dogs. There were endless eerie noises and knocks, complete with cold breezes seeming to come out of nowhere. The manor looked like a model Hollywood haunted house. Nor did it hurt to have a ghostly aura—it kept potential vandals and intruders away. As it was, the Kellers had enough problems dealing with the trashed-out, graffiti-besmirched building without handling any new invaders. Consequently, they did not deny rumors that there might be ghosts on the premises. This is unlike another prestigious bed and breakfast, the Castle Marne: it categorically refuses to host any ghosts, stating the Lumber Baron Inn is welcome to them.

(Owners of inns often find ghost hunters to be thorough nuisances. Such investigators are so intent on finding spirits with various technical equipment that they prowl through all areas of the house during the day and night. In the process, they think nothing of disturbing other guests. Drunken, profanity-filled tirades are sometimes their responses to those who question their premises and behavior.)

Among the spirits possibly present at the Lumber Baron Inn are those of Cara Lee Knoche and Marianne Weaver. Born on October 11, 1953, Knoche was a badly troubled young woman by 1970 who was living separately from her parents who dwelt in Golden. After having attended Wheat Ridge and Golden high schools the previous academic year, she had not enrolled back in school that fall. Rather, in September, she occupied a cramped, $48-dollar-a-month one-room unit on the second floor of the Mouat Mansion, sharing the space with Sharon McHome who had been there about four months. Before settling in, Knoche had been a frequent visitor to McHome's apartment.

Shortly after Knoche moved in, McHome left Denver for an extended visit to her mother in California. Others in the house, who had little contact with the tall, blonde Knoche, described her as wearing hippie clothing. Her apartment included psychedelic posters.

The 18-year-old Weaver had graduated from Bear Creek High School in June 1970, enrolling at Arapahoe Community College. Living with her parents at 2428

South Balsam Street near the Rolling Hills Country Club in Lakewood, she was a frequent visitor to Knoche's apartment. The two young women had many guests, mostly men. Loud parties in their space often went on to the small hours of the morning. Landlord Jim Fowler complained that McHome and Knoche were sometimes late in paying the rent while he warned Knoche about the parties. In response, she announced she was going to move out on Thursday, October 15. (At this time, Fowler lived off the premises at 4235 Bryant Street with Frances Fowler. That was a short-lived marriage which soon ended in divorce.)

Around 9:00 PM on Monday, October 12, Weaver left her parents' house to visit Knoche. This was the situation when, about 2:45 AM on Tuesday, October 13, John Lechuga of 3751 Navajo Street drove by the Mouat Mansion. Apparently a regular visitor to Knoche, he noticed Weaver's car parked near the house. Looking up at Knoche's room, he was surprised, despite the hour, to see the blinds pulled and the light off in her unit. Going up to investigate, he found the door ajar—he had no difficulty getting into the house. On pushing open the door to Knoche's apartment and switching on the light, he discovered the clothed murdered body of Weaver atop the bed. On the floor, partially under the bed, was the nude body of Knoche.

Rather than raising an alarm and asking for help of others in the house, Lechuga left the murder site, going to a pay phone at a restaurant near West 37th Avenue and Federal Boulevard where he called the police, telling them a fight was in progress at the dining spot. Once the police arrived, he confessed he had deliberately not told them about the killings, fearing he might be overheard. He then led the officers back to the Mouat Mansion. The authorities observed that Weaver had been shot to death with a small caliber bullet in her forehead. The murderer had strangled Knoche to death.

Evidence showed pry marks on the door as if someone had broken into the unit. Those in the house had reported that others had sought to visit Knoche's apartment that night and had been surprised to find the door locked. No one had sought to investigate the unusual circumstances.

Near the bodies was a paper bag containing marijuana and a hash pipe. While investigators scoured the crime scene, they did not find evidence linking the murders to any specific suspect. No one else in the house claimed to have heard anything. The coroner set the time of

Lumber Baron Inn

Far from being haunted, some believe the Lumber Baron Inn may be blessed with an angel. This shot is of a neighbor, playing an angel in a Christmas pageant in 1954.

Drawings by Laura Givens

Cara Knoche, left, and Marianne Weaver, were the victims of a murder at the Mouat Mansion on October 12–13, 1970. The crime has never been solved. Supposedly, their spirits haunt the Lumber Baron Inn.

the deaths between about 9:15 PM on October 12 and 2:30 AM on October 13. The presence of the marijuana/drug paraphernalia hinted it might have been a drug-related killing. Others suspected that, with the numerous male visitors, Knoche could have been running some sort of sex operation out of her apartment.

Subsequent accounts claimed the killings were the city's first official drug murders of the 1970s though, other than for the small amount of marijuana, no controlled substances were discovered on the premises. The assertion has also been made that Cara was raped before being strangled to death—there were no signs of struggle in the unit. Another version is that Weaver stumbled on the crime, leading to her slaying. A related description states that Weaver's body was found with its arms crossed over its chest, supposedly the mark of an execution. Still others argue the crossed arms are a message of remorse.

Within days of the murder, the police interviewed more than 50 people. Among them were associates of Knoche and Weaver who volunteered information. Weaver's father, who stated he had expected his daughter to be back by 12:30 AM, had not acted to find where she was when she did not come home as expected. Before embracing the hippie lifestyle, Marianne had been active for about seven years in the Lakewood Westernaires, a group of teenage girls who rode and performed on horses. The Denver-born victim had turned 18 on August 27, 1970, having met Cara about two to three years before her fatal visit to the Mouat Mansion. She was buried at Mount Olivet Cemetery. Marianne left behind an infant daughter.

Cara had last visited her parents on her 17th birthday, October 11. She was in good spirits, reporting she had found a new apartment, never having been completely comfortable at the Mouat Mansion. Born in Salt Lake City and raised in Denver, she had been working at a car wash at the time of her death. Interment was in the Arvada Cemetery.

A search of the apartment found a discharged shell from a .22 revolver. The apartment was rife with identifiable fingerprints. None of them, however, could be linked to the crimes. Nor were the authorities able to discover a murder weapon. The homicides have never been solved. The lead detective in the case, Jack Isenhart, later became head of security for Regis University. Before his death, he occasionally called on the Lumber Baron Inn, sharing memories about the case in the hope that it might someday be broken.

After the Lumber Baron Inn opened, despite the first-class renovation, there were still strange creaks and cold spots within it. During severe wind storms, the wind whistled around the house. At times, people have felt there is something or somebody hovering near them in the Valentine Suite, the room in which Knoche and Weaver were murdered.

For a while, the inn teamed up with Ghost Hunter's University. This was a commercial venture arguing that modern scientific technology could detect and

Photo by Jody Scatto

Ghost hunters claim to have found the image of the pictured Victorian schoolmarm, inset, haunting the Lumber Baron Inn to the left of the curtains in the mirror above the fireplace in the front parlor.

understand beings from other worlds and dimensions. To help the curious learn the lore, Ghost Hunter's University held national seminars, including "Ghost Hunting 101." Meetings at the Lumber Baron Inn often included a meal and a chance to probe whether there might be something to the assertions of the professional ghost hunters. *Haunted Times*, a magazine linked to Ghost Hunter's University, featured the turret of the Lumber Baron Inn on its cover as part of the publication's nameplate.

Certified ghost hunters claim to have discovered all sorts of strange images at the Lumber Baron Inn. In the out-of-focus shot on the right, for example, they see a black cat perched on the transom window of the Valentine Suite during an investigation of the Mouat Mansion on Friday, October 13, 2000, the night of a full moon which was the 30th anniversary of the murder of Cara Knoche and Marianne Weaver. Below, is the eerie coal tunnel in the basement, a space a psychic described as a "room within a room," possibly complete with bones which might have once been buried there.

both Lumber Baron Inn

Generally, ghost nights, which continued after the passing of Ghost Hunter's University, last about three hours. During the first thirty minutes, Walter Keller and others tell ghost stories about the place. Participants then use the ghost-hunting devices in the hope of explaining the mysteries. Among them is whether the spirit of John Mouat is present. Something of a Scottish puritan, he did not like the liquor trade. Perhaps his specter is protesting the serving of alcohol at the bed and breakfast.

A woman popping up on the landing of the grand staircase is another Lumber Baron Inn phantom. People walking in the foyer, including Walter, sometimes get

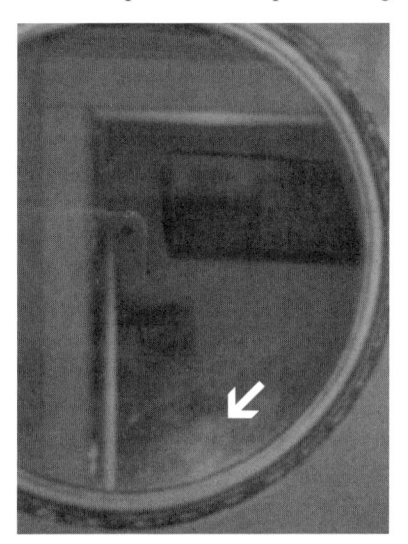

both Lumber Baron Inn

The shadow of murder victim Marianne Weaver is in the circular mirror in the Lumber Baron Inn's Helen Keller Suite. At least ghost hunters see as much in this blurry image on the left. Others believe it is the shade of Cara Lee Knoche, the other young woman killed in the Mouat Mansion. Ghost hunters, below, use a wide array of cameras and fancy technological devices in the hope of discovering spirits. Here they probe the ballroom of the Lumber Baron Inn in 2005 as part of a program sponsored by Ghost Hunter's University, an organization formed by Christopher Moon.

the feeling they are being watched. Looking up, they observe the apparition, dressed in Victorian garb with her hair primly done in a bun, staring at them. Since the shade has something of a scolding, schoolmarm look, some think she might have been a teacher at Denver Business University. On occasion, the wood on the staircase appears to move under the presence of the specter. Believers in phantoms also insist the schoolmarm's shadow pops up in the mantel mirror above the fireplace in the front parlor.

Ghost researchers have also claimed to have discovered electronic voice phenomena on recordings, including of disembodied utterances and sounds. Among them is a screeching cat though the Lumber Baron Inn has never had a cat on the premises. Some assert they have viewed a ghostly reflection in a mirror that resembles murder victim Marianne Weaver. Others have dismissed this as the product of overwrought imaginations. For example, occasional flashing lights in the mansion are actually the product of magic tricks, part of performances at various mur-

Lumber Baron Inn

Spirit P.I. is a ghost-hunting team that has conducted dozens of searches for specters in the Lumber Baron Inn. Its head, Kevin Sampron, is in the right foreground of his crew at the bottom of the mansion's main staircase. An orb is on his shirt beneath his right shoulder.

der mysteries and other entertainments. Frequently, the Lumber Baron has magic shows on Thursday evenings.

Still, ghost yarns have been persistent. There is the tale of a woman in a blue flapper dress from the 1920s. One time, the mother of a bride, preparing for the wedding at the Lumber Baron Inn, saw the apparition sitting on a ledge by a window in the ballroom with glass of champagne in hand. Despite a no-smoking policy in the house, some have smelled the odor of cigarettes after glancing at the apparition of the flapper.

During a ghost hunt on Friday, October 13, 2000, the night of a full moon which was the thirtieth anniversary of the murder of Cara Knoche and Marianne

Weaver, psychics claimed to have discovered the image of a black cat sitting atop the transom window of the Valentine Suite. For a while, John Keller had his own personal ghost, "Nicey Nice," in his basement room at the Lumber Baron Inn. He described it as a teenage boy, complete with a gray complexion and yellow nose. Every morning it greeted him, saying hello.

Such groups as Spirit P.I., led by Kevin Sampron, have conducted dozens of searches in the house, insisting they have discovered orbs on photos they have then taken. APG, the Altitude Paranormal Group, has overseen Lumber Baron Inn ghost nights in recent years. Led by Grayson McGraw, it claims to have captured the facsimile of the flapper ghost in the ballroom.

Lumber Baron Inn

Haunted Times *featured the Lumber Baron Inn on its cover to the left of its name.*

On Halloween, besides candy, the Lumber Baron Inn hands out a flyer that includes a ghost story, a word puzzle, and a coloring book space. Many parents then descend on the bed and breakfast with their children. About that time of year, the bed and breakfast has also hosted some ghost tours—over the years, Walter has led assorted walks around town. Realizing that many of the notorious spooks of North Denver live considerably away from the bed and breakfast, it invites them over for the occasion. So it is that it tells the story of Denver's Spider Man.

Theodore Coneys was a 59-year-old drifter in 1941 who had grown up in the Mile High City before hitting the road in the early 20th century. He was a longtime friend of the 73-year-old Philip Peters of 3335 West Moncrieff Place. This was the situation on a cold day that fall when Coneys, recently returned to Denver from a tramp in upstate New York, called on Peters. Discovering no one at home, Coneys broke into the house and raided the refrigerator. He then discovered a tiny cubbyhole in the attic where he spent the night. Coneys was comfortable there. Before long, like a spider, he constantly went up and down from his hidden compartment. When Peters finally discovered him on October 17, 1941, Coneys viciously beat Peters to death, hiding out in the attic until he was finally captured on July 30, 1942. The press branded the lanky six-foot, two-inch, 95-pound Coneys "Spider Man." Ever since, he has been at the center of countless North Denver haunted house tales.

Lumber Baron Inn

Ghosts and spirits come together at the Lumber Baron Inn. Here shadows and shades appear to pop up as a visitor holds a bottle of wine. Psychics especially claim to see a spectral illusion at the far right of the mirror. This picture was taken by an overnight guest who had checked into the bed and breakfast in the hope of having a haunting experience.

The Lumber Baron Inn has also welcomed spirits from Acacia Cemetery. In 1866, working with the Odd Fellows, the Masons laid out the burial grounds between West 26th and West 32nd avenues from the equivalent of Tejon Street to Zuni Street as a romantic final resting place for members of the orders. While interments began in May of the next year, Acacia Cemetery was never lushly landscaped. Most of the bodies were subsequently moved. Even so, over the years, excavations have revealed bones, complete with rumors that ghosts remain from the necropolis. John Mouat had been a Mason.

Those not liking or wanting specters have urged them to go to the Lumber Baron Inn. People at North High, for example, have offered the bed and breakfast all of the school's alleged spirits. At times, ghosts have been a convenient excuse for some of the problems of the Mouat Mansion. On a less than memorable Valentine's Day, with a full house and special events that evening, suddenly the hot water heater went out. Not everybody accepted the excuse that the Lumber Baron Inn did not want its guests to get in hot water for the celebration.

Murder Mystery Dinners

In addition to being a romantic place to stay and the city's premier spot for weddings, the Lumber Baron Inn draws many visitors to its Murder Mystery Dinners. These are interactive evenings where the audience witnesses and helps solve a sensational crime while simultaneously enjoying dinner and meeting others at group tables.

When Walter Keller was creating the Lumber Baron Inn, he knew it would be as much an events center as a traditional bed and breakfast. Even so, he was not sure of precisely the scope and the nature of the events it would host. Both by chance and heritage, the murder mysteries became a prime part of the facility.

Shortly after the Lumber Baron opened in September 1994, it hosted a holiday dinner for a telecommunications firm. The company featured a murder mystery as the entertainment. Marne Wills-Cuellar staged the show as part of her Marne International Productions. She was an actress who literally had something of a bag of tricks. In this case, it was a trunk of props she and her cast brought with them to the Lumber Baron Inn. At the appropriate time, they donned their costumes. As the story was unfolding, suddenly a key figure was murdered. Clues were placed around the ballroom which diners studied during intermission. After the break, a traditional sleuth in the mold of Sherlock Holmes or Inspector Hercule Poirot took charge. Evaluating the evidence and interviewing suspects and witnesses, he temporarily appeared stumped. He called on the audience to help him. People at various tables worked as teams, coming up with their conclusion as to who done it. Finally, putting everything together, the detective nabbed the guilty party.

The mystery dinner was not only a hit for those attending the holiday affair, but the Lumber Baron Inn soon got calls about when it was next going to host a comparable evening. This led Keller to contact Marne and her husband, Carlos Cuellar, a veteran salesman. Before long, Walter had a working relationship with the couple, staging about five to ten shows in 1995. By 1996, the number was up to 20 to 25,

Lumber Baron Inn

In early 2008, Icing BrideZilla *was the Lumber Baron Inn's first in-house murder mystery. It went over so well the company has revived it annually.*

usually once every other week. Marne handled the productions, Walter tended bar and oversaw marketing. After a while, Marne also took care of ticketing. An outside caterer was responsible for the meals.

As the murder mysteries were becoming increasingly part of the Lumber Baron Inn's identity, Walter was driving by the house where he grew up at 2338 Federal Boulevard in 2006 when he noticed a for sale sign at the adjacent corner at 2406 Federal Boulevard. This was a one-time elite single-family house which had long been a mortuary. During his youth, Walter had shoveled the walk there and had been allowed to explore the interior of the funeral home. On visiting the vacant building with a Realtor, he immediately envisaged how he could transform the space into an ideal spot for murder mysteries.

On this basis, going into partnership with Marne and Carlos, and guaranteeing the bank loan through the equity of the Lumber Baron Inn, he helped the couple obtain a loan from the Mayor's Office of Economic Development. This led to the opening of the Adams Mystery Playhouse. At Walter's suggestion, it featured the Casket Bar, the Seance Parlor, a spiderweb floor, and a large sign featuring a detective's eye staring through a magnifying glass. Keller used his own eye as the model for the logo. He drew on his old neighborhood ties to convince locals to support a zoning change and liquor license for the new establishment.

Walter was frequently at the Adams Mystery Playhouse, helping promote the shows. This led the Lumber Baron Inn to quit featuring murder mysteries. About this time, 2007, Walter put the Lumber Baron Inn on the market, buying a house near Sloans Lake while he hoped to make a new career in theater as part of the

Adams Mystery Playhouse. Before this could materialize, with virtually no explanation, Marne and Carlos told Walter he was no longer welcome at their establishment. Realizing a legal fight with them would be emotionally draining, he walked away from the Adams Mystery Playhouse. His investment there was something of an apprenticeship in the field of how to produce and create murder mysteries.

Simultaneously, the real estate market collapsed with the financial troubles of 2008 whereby Walter saw that the Lumber Baron Inn was his destiny. Even before the financial crisis, Walter had reestablished murder mysteries at the Lumber Baron Inn. He vowed to give them a racier edge than anything staged by Marne and Carlos. Here and there, he threw in topical political barbs. Purchasing professional props and emphasizing a sound system, he vowed the Murder Mystery Dinners would be bigger, better productions than what the Lumber Baron Inn had previously hosted.

From the beginning, Keller's wife Julie was his close partner in the effort. In the fall of 2007, they were finally able to take a real honeymoon. The couple vacationed in Mexico—they had purchased the trip at a silent auction raising funds for a charity. There they devised *Icing BrideZilla: Wedding to Die*, as much a farce as a traditional murder mystery. Aiming at cutting-edge humor and containing

Photo by Phil Goodstein

Members of the audience participate in mystery dinners at the Lumber Baron Inn, often wearing masks and costumes. Stephanie Bruce, a regular in the company performing at the bed and breakfast, holds the microphone. Another member of the cast, Matt Brandt, is on the far right.

Magic acts are frequently part of Lumber Baron Inn murder mysteries. Here Dave Elstun performs. He styles himself a disciple of acclaimed conjurer Dai Vernon.

sexual innuendo, they cast Walter as the big, extremely ugly bride, Kamilla Rugburn, who was set to marry a robot. The show started as a traditional wedding reception. Right amidst the nuptials, suddenly Kamilla was murdered.

Rusty Schwinn, played by Walter, showed up on his rusty Schwinn to solve the homicide. He is a member of the Denver Police Bike Squad, known by insiders as "B.S." It is not to be confused with the actual police bicycle patrol. While the show tried to have a link between the clues and the solution of the crime, in subsequent shows, all written by Walter and Julie, the connection was often nebulous. Now and then, members of the audience have accused Rusty Schwinn of being the killer. The plays are far more comedies than tragedies. On occasion, a sensational theft rather than a killing is at the heart of the mystery.

Theater runs in Keller's blood. His grandparents in Missouri had participated in minstrel shows. The evenings are also designed to pull in the audience. Participation of members of the crowd is vital to making the productions come alive. To assure this is the case, the Lumber Baron Inn screens ticketbuyers, scouting out volunteers. When patrons reserve space, it seeks to learn more about them, especially if they are attending in groups and celebrating a birthday or anniversary. The show might be specially slanted to highlight such an event. Now and then, the Lumber Baron Inn finds an audience volunteer so witty and appealing that it approaches the would-be actor, seeing if he is interested in being a regular at the murder mysteries.

Walter's son John has been part of the murder mysteries. In addition to sometimes performing in them, the young man has proven to be a technical wizard in helping produce the shows. Already when he was nine years old, he suggested a projection system to enhance the special effects and give the audience a better idea of the clues and the suspects. John has frequently operated the sound and light system during the performances. After attending Sandoval School and Skinner Middle School, he enhanced his education in the field by studying in the video-cinema arts division of the highly acclaimed Denver School of the Arts, a magnet high school for students gifted in the performance and graphic arts.

Now and then, showgirls pop up in murder mysteries dressed in ornate costumes seemingly from the world of acclaimed actress, singer, and producer Bette Midler. This is not a coincidence. Julie is an avid supporter of Midler's New York Restoration Project, an effort to plant trees and recreate the glory of forgotten and neglected urban parks. With Walter, she visits New York annually for the charity's major fundraising affair. They have gone to some of Midler's events in Las Vegas. The Lumber Baron Inn has obtained costumes and props linked to Midler's performances.

To appeal to a wide array of patrons, the Lumber Baron Inn presents a variety of shows. Among them is Gambling Night. For the occasion, the Lumber Baron

Lumber Baron Inn

Some of the actresses in murder mystery presentations wear costumes fresh from Las Vegas. They are products of the friendship between Julie and Walter Keller with acclaimed entertainer Bette Midler. Here they are together in a fundraiser on September 20, 2009.

Members of the audience intently study the clues during a murder mystery.

Inn sets up its parlors to resemble a casino, complete with tables and house chips which it purchased from a defunct casino-dealing school. Around Christmas, it especially emphasizes its casino holiday parties. At other times, the bed and breakfast features "Sleightly Impossible Magic," where a magic act is central to the mystery evening. All are part of what it calls "After-Dinnertainment."

Members of the audience frequently include guests at the bed and breakfast—the Lumber Baron Inn offers visitors special deals on the plays. The shows feature general, deluxe, and VIP seats. Those purchasing the latter two categories are given tokens entitling them to a free drink or some of the merchandise displayed in the front parlor of the Lumber Baron Inn after the shows. A repeat business is part of the success of the Murder Mystery Dinners.

The Mystery Mansion's Playbill

Icing BrideZilla: A Murder Mystery Wedding Reception. Opened January 2008.

Campaigns Are Murder: A Murder Mystery Dinner. Opened August 2008.

Casino Night Heist: A Casino Mystery Dinner. Opened November 2008.

Inn Over His Head: A Role-Playing Murder Mystery Dinner. Opened March 2009.

Haunted House Hunt: A Ghost-Story Murder Mystery Dinner. Opened September 2009.

The Vanishing Act: A Magic Murder Mystery Dinner. Opened October 2009.

Shooting Double Down Donny: A Movie-Making Casino Murder Mystery. Opened December 2009.

Lumber Baron Inn

The actors and actresses who have performed in murder mysteries at the Lumber Baron Inn beginning in 2008: **Back row (top),** *from left to right: Mike Heckel, Walter Keller, John Keller, Stephanie Bruce, Trevor Huster, Julie Keller, Michala Hardesty, Tim Housand, Amber Davis, Dave Elstun.* **Middle row**: *Michele Heckel, Cameron Truesdale, Brittney Hanze, Darrin Ray, Matt Vander Meulen, Scott Glennon, Ember Everett, Laura Powers, Isobel McGowan.* **Front row (bottom)**: *Brandon K. Parker, Gene Gordon, Matt Brandt, Elizabeth Gallegos, Anthony Adams, Samantha Storm (tech), Sara Kerlin, Marq Del Monte, Gwenelle Buzick.*

America's Got Murder: A Talent Show Murder Mystery Dinner. Opened June 2010.

Sequel To Murder (*Double Down Donny 2*): A Movie-Making Casino Murder Mystery. Opened November 2010

Murder at the Shakespeare Chateau: A Murder Mystery Dinner. Opened April 2012.

Let's Kill the Whistle-blower: A Casino Murder Mystery Dinner. Opening November 2013

ᴀ Visit to the Lumber Baron Inn

The Lumber Baron Inn is designed to recreate a visit to a grand Victorian manor, whisking guests to the world of the 1890s. The front door alone says this. Instead of a keypad or a modern security system, it depends on vintage keys. Quaint skeleton keys provide entry into the house. This is but the beginning.

John Mouat placed his crest on the main chimney of his mansion.

The front porch of the Mouat Mansion disappeared somewhere between 1943 and 1945 as illustrated by these two photos taken in front of the house.

On checking in, guests receive a tour of the house. The Lumber Baron Inn also gives them dinner recommendations, telling them about the wide variety of local restaurants. The visitor additionally learns about breakfast choices. The options are joining a group meal in the dining room hosted by Walter, a private table, weather permitting, on the front porch, or a room-service meal. Some, especially newlyweds and those on romantic getaways, prefer the last. Breakfast is a full meal, complete with fruit, a hot entrée with eggs and meat, baked goods, juice, and other beverages. The inn provides vegetarian meals if requested. It makes special arrangements for those unable to come to the scheduled breakfast times of 8:00, 8:30, and 9:00 AM.

Though proud of being something of a time machine transporting visitors to a previous era, the Lumber Baron Inn has had to adopt to modern times. For example, when John Mouat occupied the mansion, the house did not have a big iron fence surrounding it. The barrier was necessary for security reasons, especially when the house was being renovated. It also provides a sense of space and privacy.

A big plasma flatscreen is on the wall of the back parlor. While, at first glance, it is out of place in a bed and breakfast selling itself as an idyllic escape, it reflects 21st-century customs and demands. The Lumber Baron Inn hosts numerous community and business events. Some of those participating at them find having such a screen absolutely necessary for their presentations. The lodge uses the screen for assorted sales promotions. Guests wishing to keep up with developments in the world appreciate the flatscreen televisions in their rooms. The screen in the back parlor, incidentally, is right above the antique organ of Walter's grandmother which he brought to the Lumber Baron Inn from St. Joseph, Missouri.

Lumber Baron Inn, above; photo by Phil Goodstein below

Adding a new wraparound back porch was part of the renovation of the Mouat Mansion into the Lumber Baron Inn.

The Lumber Baron Inn is a premier spot for weddings in its large yard/garden.

The original front porch wrapped around much of the south and east sides of the house. Until the advent of air conditioning, porches were part and parcel of urban living. They provided a place where people took in the air. Additionally, they provided a great socializing space. Neighbors frequently visited on the porch while residents greeted locals walking through the area.

Porches require maintenance. An owner's neglect of a house is often most visible on the porch. Slowly the veranda decays. Sometimes, with shifting of the ground, it becomes separated from the residence. Then, rather than investing to repair and restore the porch, those owning properties for exclusive immediate economic gain sometimes rip them out. The Mouat porch disappeared somewhere between 1943 and 1945. A small, simple staircase led from the ground to the main entry.

A replacement of the porch as it originally looked was a prime part of the restoration of the mansion. The remodeling also saw the adding of a new rear porch, one the Lumber Baron Inn combined with a side veranda to provide for a wheelchair ramp. Since it leads directly into the kitchen, guests do not regularly use the back porch. Even so, it connects the house with the garden. In rebuilding the back porch, the Kellers found just enough of the original design and decorations to get them reproduced to give the deck a Victorian charm. (When the fir floor of the rebuilt front porch started to splinter badly after about ten years, the Lumber Baron Inn rebuilt the deck with reconstituted plastic compound. The lumber floor of the back porch was more substantially constructed and has held up much better.)

The grand oak front door is illustrative of John Mouat's skills as a carpenter. It features an ornate cut of tiger striping whereby the bright wood jumps out at the visitor. The tiger striping is so carefully banded into the rest of the thick twin doors that it is difficult to see exactly how it is attached to the doors. Possibly, it was cut into them. Rounded brick is next to the door.

Ornate, silver-plated hinges connect the doors to the wall. Originally, all of the hardware at the front entry was silver plated. A stone carving of the Mouat crest is on the main chimney. It includes thistle leaves, a saw, and other carpenter tools.

Between the exterior front doors and the house proper is a small vestibule. It provides a space to protect the interior from sudden changes in weather and temperature on the opening of the front door. Elegant oak paneling ascends to the ceiling. In some ways, the vestibule is the most authentic room in the Mouat Mansion since it was never remodeled for residential purposes. Even so, a tiled nameplate has seemingly disappeared from the floor of the entry.

A maid or butler answered the door at a mansion in the late 19th/early 20th century. The servant welcomed the caller to the house, asking him to stay in the front room while taking the visitor's card to the person for whom it was intended.

Photo by Phil Goodstein

The front door of the Mouat Mansion features ornate tiger striping next to rounded bricks.

The alcove of the Mouat Mansion was particularly a showroom. It was something of an advertisement of the intricate architecture and design of the house, complete with pocket doors, carved rosettes, and brilliant wallpaper.

John Mouat built his mansion right when the English arts and crafts movement was impacting all aspects of American interior household design. Especially treasured were ornate wallpapers. The Lumber Baron Inn commissioned Bradbury & Bradbury Art Wallpaper of California to design distinctive wallpapers for the restored inn. They have special themes in each room. In the entry foyer, for example, are Anglo-Japanese prints. They match the frieze. The ceiling paper features birds fluttering about.

Photo by Phil Goodstein, above; below, Lumber Baron Inn

The front parlor of the Lumber Baron Inn, above, features an ornate fireplace mantel. Bradbury & Bradbury designed the mansion's wallpaper. Below Peter Bridgeman installs the wallpaper in the Honeymoon Suite.

Frosted glass in the interior door has a similar theme with images of flying birds. The original glass was among the many gems of the house that were badly vandalized or stolen. Part of the remnants of the glass was damaged by a bullet hole. The entry room further features the exquisite grand oak staircase anchored by a commanding newel, complete with a carved thistle leaf. This is a sign of Mouat's Scottish heritage. He installed comparable newels in other large houses he built. When the mansion was divided into apartments, four separate bathrooms occupied the space that the Lumber Baron Inn has restored as the entry room. (Years after opening the lodge, with the help of Dave Cole, Walter cut into the newel, hoping to find John Mouat's building plans. There was nothing there.)

Off to the left of the foyer is

Photo by Walter Keller

A carved newel anchors the grand staircase in the entry room of the Mouat Mansion.

the front parlor. Ten-foot-high pocket doors separate it from the entry room. Another set of pocket doors divide the front parlor from the back parlor. There were diverse uses of the parlors depending on families. In some places, there was a men's parlor as opposed to a women's parlor, the sexes segregating themselves after dinner. In other places, there was a day parlor complemented by an evening parlor. It is not exactly clear how the Mouat family used the large spaces. In addition to entertaining on the first floor, the Mouats also hosted events on the third floor in the ballroom.

During the mansion's long epoch as a rather unkempt apartment house, the pocket doors were sealed off or closed tight. The ones by the main entry were hung upside-down as a wall separating the front parlor, an individual unit, from the entry room. Doors were cut through this "wall" leading to the hall and a bathroom. A complete restoration of the pocket doors is an ongoing goal of the continued improvement and enhancement of the house.

The front parlor features cherry wood with the fleur-de-lis in the rosettes. Hanging near the main fireplace are pictures of John and Amelia Mouat, provided by members of the Mouat family. The room also includes the turret. The Lumber Baron Inn has used the space for a grand piano that seemingly performs by itself—it is designed with the modern player piano technology to play an inserted disc.

This shot, taken from near the back parlor fireplace, shows the dining room to the left, entry room in the center, and front parlor on the right.

The chandeliers are not authentic. Mouat built the house when gas and electricity were competing for dominance as the preferred means of household illumination. There were both tubes for the gas and space for wiring in the original lighting fixtures. Amazingly, there were few fires caused by the close proximity of gas and rather primitive wiring. The gas lines were capped during the early 20th century when electricity definitely asserted itself as the more reliable and economic source of lighting interior spaces. Here and there, remnants of the gas lines are still in place, especially above the first floor ceiling.

Ceiling medallions are missing from above the chandeliers. These were ornate plaster-cast implements directly above the lighting standards. Dating from the time when candles were the primary source of illumination of European palaces, they were designed to resist the flames and smoke. An exploration of the ceilings of the Mouat Mansion has not shown any evidence of such medallions. The Lumber Baron Inn includes elaborately shaped ceiling paper patterns where the medallions would have been in a traditional Victorian manor.

Nor is the throne authentic. This is the huge chair positioned near the front parlor fireplace. Indonesian craftsmen created the intricate piece in the late 20th century. The Lumber Baron Inn acquired it from a local antique dealer. It took all of the moving crew's skills to wedge it through the front door of the house. The seat is a favorite place where visitors pose for memorable photos.

The pocket doors work between the front and back parlors. The hardware on them features the original pattern, something of a sunburst theme. The doors allow for both separating and combining functions on the main floor.

Sycamore fills the back parlor. The replacement mantel, which dates from about the beginning of the 20th century, is of gum wood. The back door, by the pocket doors leading to the dining room, has been repositioned. It was another of the many strange cuts and modifications of the original layout of the house. The back parlor is a popular space for forums and meetings.

Oak paneling highlights the dining room. The chamber originally included a buzzer in the floor near the main seat so those present could call the waiter. An early modification of the Mouat Mansion was the removal of the servant bells.

Dining room rosettes feature cherries, plums, apples, grapes, and acorns. The stained glass over the back bar is a replacement, designed to accentuate the dining atmosphere. A piece of fretwork was once close to where the Lumber Baron Inn installed the bar. It was among the many fixtures that were badly damaged.

The fireplace mantel is another replacement of a prime missing fixture. Apparently, there was originally a large, double mantel reputed to feature fruits comparable to those highlighted on the rosettes. Around the fireplace is inlaid tiling. The pieces in it are both replacements and originals. Dogs chasing deer was a theme of the design when the Mouats were in the house. When Walter Keller first saw the house, tiles were scattered about the floor of the room. Later, another person who had viewed the house returned some of the tile she had then picked up from the landmark.

The dining room connects with the office of the Lumber Baron Inn. Once the library of the Mouat Mansion, it had been a kitchen for the unit which occupied the

Photo by Brittney Hanze

Gamblers pose at the roulette table in the front parlor of the Lumber Baron Inn during a Casino Night.

Photo by Tom Torgove

*A rack modeled on a harp is in the Lumber Baron Inn's Honeymoon Suite.
It was originally designed to show confidential attire at a Victoria's Secret.*

dining room. That apartment, incidentally, had a Murphy bed. There were also folding beds in the third-floor apartments and likely elsewhere in the house.

A spiral staircase leads from the office to the basement. It is not original. The banister was initially in the Queen of Heaven Orphanage, a facility near the northwest corner of West 48th Avenue and Federal Boulevard run by the Missionary Sisters of the Sacred Heart for girls from two to 15 years of age. St. Mother Frances Cabrini established the facility in 1906. A four-story neo-classical brick building followed 11 years later. In 1973, the structure came down. At one time, the staircase had been where the nuns called roll at night, assuring that all the wards were in their rooms. The Lumber Baron Inn obtained the banister via the Herman Heiser House at 3016 Osceola Street when David and Barb Sheldon sold that landmark. Barb Sheldon had been a foremost mentor to Keller about the problems and potentials of historic preservation.

Initially, there was no basement connection from the room that is the Lumber Baron Inn's office. The staircase has the aura of something of a secret passageway. Walter takes delight in sometimes descending into the basement in the office only quickly to appear on the other side of the house. Any old mansion, he observes, needs some sort of hidden space.

Opposite the door leading to the office is the first-floor bathroom. The latter was once the butler's pantry, connecting the dining room with the kitchen. It also included a laundry chute which went down to the basement. Compared to the numerous toilets in modern houses, they were amazingly rare in Victorian manors. There was only one full bathroom in the original Mouat Mansion. Generally, people bathed but once a week. Bodily functions were considered so unmentionable at the time that it was generally considered impolite to ask about restroom facilities. Most likely, there was a first-floor toilet in addition to one in the basement.

The back part of the house was not nearly as lavishly designed as the public and family living quarters. The lumber is softwood. There is a back servants' stairway, one which has been rebuilt with oak. The kitchen is a modern commercial operation where cooks can fix anything from a simple breakfast to a banquet. Usually, Julie Keller prepares the meals, being presented to those attending mystery dinners as "Chef Sue Flay." A hand-operated dumbwaiter transports food and dishes between the kitchen and the third-floor ballroom.

The second floor was the family floor with bedrooms and the only true bathroom of the original Mouat Mansion. The Honeymoon Suite is the premier place for guests. It is two rooms, with 11-foot-high ceilings, separated by pocket doors. Besides a king-sized bed and a ceiling-length mirror, it features a sitting room with

Photo by Tom Torgove

The dining room of the Mouat Mansion includes a wine cabinet, a tiled fireplace, mantel, and stained glass.

an old-fashioned fainting couch. A Jacuzzi occupies the turret, providing for inti-
macy and a most romantic experience.

The towel rack in the Honeymoon Suite resembles a life-sized orchestral harp. It was
originally designed to show intimate apparel at a Victoria's Secret. Adding to the sexy
allure is that, on occasion, the Lumber Baron Inn has hosted boudoir photo sessions.

Photos by Kent Meireis ©

These fisheye photos of the Valentine Suite, above, and the Colonel Franklin Room
illustrate the romantic layout of Lumber Baron Inn guest rooms.

Apparently, the Honeymoon Suite was originally part of the three-room master suite of the Mouat Mansion. During the epoch when the house was carved into numerous apartments, a staircase cut through part of the main bedroom to the third floor. The other room of the master suite has become the Colonel Franklin Room.

This is the Lumber Baron Inn's smallest visitor room, designed for a business traveler. It remembers Walter's father, Colonel Franklin Keller. Some of the airman's military memorabilia are on display there. Originally, the suite was named for a perceived distant Keller relative, Charles S. Thomas (1849–1934), a most influential attorney who was Colorado governor from 1899 to 1901 and in the United States Senate from 1913 to 1921.

As in the rest of the house, the Lumber Baron Inn had to replace the mantel and restore the tile work around the fireplace in the Colonel Franklin Room. In this case, it managed to obtain the pollard oak mantel from San Francisco. The tiles are from a demolished Capitol Hill mansion.

The Valentine Suite is next to the Honeymoon Suite. Again, a mixture of antiques and modern conveniences are keynotes of the room. Besides suggesting romance, the name recalls John Mouat's daughter Margaret Valentine. Her girlhood picture is above the fireplace mantel. As with other rooms in the house, the suite features diamond-cut bevel leaded glass. At the right time of the day, a rainbow shines in the room when the sunlight hits the window.

Margaret, who was still alive when the renovation of the Mouat Mansion began, was an enthusiast of Asian art and culture. Recognizing this, the Lumber Baron Inn designed the room with an exotic Persian theme. Showing the diversity of the house and Asia, it includes a teak Indonesian wedding bed.

Across the hall is the Anniversary Suite. It has a Greco-Roman theme, complete with a restored fireplace and a couple of tin porch pillars designed to look like classical marble columns. Its bathroom was once two separate restrooms. Most likely, that was the site of the Mouat Mansion's bathroom. As with all of the other bedrooms, the Anniversary Suite includes an archway used as a shower. John Mouat often placed such archways in the houses he built. They were the locations of plumbed marble sinks in his manor.

The Lumber Baron Inn once had a fifth guest room, the Helen Keller Suite. It honored the famous blind-deaf activist and humanitarian who lived from 1880 to 1968. She was another distant Keller relative. Walter and Julie have occupied it as their room—after their marriage, Julie insisted on moving upstairs, not wishing to "live like a mole" in the basement.

When the Mouats dwelt in the mansion, they used the third floor as both servants' quarters and a ballroom. The Lumber Baron Inn has emphasized the latter use with a 1,600-square foot public space under a 20-foot-high pyramid-shaped ceiling. It has the capacity for groups of up to 90 people. The floor is maple. It came from a demolished school gymnasium in the tiny town of Chappell, Nebraska. Workers placed it above the original fir ballroom floor.

The ballroom fireplace is not original. The antique bird's-eye maple mantel might stem from the demolished David Moffat Mansion at Seventh Avenue and Grant Street. Over the years, the mantel had been modified to look like cherrywood.

Neoclassical wallpaper comparable to that in the Anniversary Suite highlights walls and the ceiling of the ballroom.

A small, intimate sitting room is in the turret adjacent to the ballroom. It has been a place where those attending parties and receptions socialize. As the Lumber Baron Inn has increasingly emphasized Murder Mystery Dinners, the inn has primarily used the sitting room as a backstage prep room, complete with costumes. Members of the audience, who volunteer for bit parts, are often taken there to be fitted up for their roles.

Echoes and reverberations sound on the third floor. In places, there is an excellent view of the mountains and a stunning vista of the skyline. It is also possible to see Denver International Airport from the top of the house. One who observed this was Mayor Wellington Webb when he visited the Lumber Baron Inn shortly after the bed and breakfast began operations in 1994. This was at a time massive bad publicity about cost overruns and a delayed opening of the airport plagued the mayor because of a dysfunctional baggage system.

As part of an effort at preserving Denver's past, Walter Keller obtained a Disneyesque star that had once shone atop the sign in front of Celebrity Lanes at 888 South Colorado Boulevard. He has placed it in the widow's walk atop the turret, right above the sitting room.

Opened on September 17, 1960, Celebrity Lanes was the city's ultimate baby-boomer play resort. Run by the Disney Corporation, the facility, also known as the Celebrity Fun Center and Celebrity Sports Center, included a huge indoor swim-

Lumber Baron Inn

The ballroom is on the third floor of the Lumber Baron Inn. The fireplace mantel on the right supposedly came from the home of David Moffat at Seventh Avenue and Grant Street.

Photo by Phil Goodstein left; courtesy Bill Wiederspan right

The top star from the sign of the demolished Celebrity Lanes, an ornate recreation center at 888 South Colorado Boulevard, is atop the turret of the Lumber Baron Inn.

ming pool, 80 lanes of bowling, a game room, slot-car racing tracks, special dining areas, and numerous other attractions which many youngsters could not resist. The modernist stars outside looked like something directly from Disneyland.

Disney sold Celebrity in 1979. Impacted by changing ownership, problematic real estate deals, and the aging of the babyboomers and their maturing passions, Celebrity was losing money by the 1990s. This led to its shuttering on June 15, 1994. The complex soon came down for a big-box building supply store. To recall Celebrity and add yet another distinctive feature to the Lumber Baron Inn, Keller procured the star. During the Christmas season, he hangs stars from the house's chandeliers which vaguely resemble the Celebrity star. *Casino Night Heist*, a mystery dinner, is in the "Celebrity Star Casino." At times, the star rotates atop the turret.

The Mouat Mansion is Denver. Its changing usages have reflected all aspects of the city. The house shows the Mile High City as a town of opportunity, a place where entrepreneurs have been able to make great fortunes. The manor also reflects the city's boom-and-bust cycle and the way the wealthy have sometimes lost most of their possessions. As Denver Business University, the palace illustrated a commitment to learning. Under the Fowler family, it represented Denver from the bottom up, both the idealism of Jim Fowler and the less than ideal conditions in which many people have lived. As the Lumber Baron Inn, it has added excitement, fancy and fantasy, mystery and romance, spirits and substance, giving people a chance both to appreciate historic preservation and the community which has nurtured it.

Acknowledgments and Sources

In the week of trauma following 9/11, many wanted to escape the constant fear and turmoil. Some were convinced that it was best simply to continue to do business as usual and stage previously planned events. Such was the case with an aspiring, politically connected law firm, Foster Graham & Huttner. Before the assault, it had sent out invitations celebrating its new office at 1226 Bannock Street. I knew Mike Huttner of the partnership from my writing about Denver's haunted houses. He had especially helped me research the Mile High dimension of *The Changeling* for my *Ghosts of Denver: Capitol Hill*.

Among the first people I encountered on entering the affair was Walter Keller. I recognized his name as a young entrepreneur who had transformed a dilapidated North Denver mansion into a sparkling bed and breakfast, the Lumber Baron Inn. My *Denver in Our Time* had mentioned the place, observing that it had once been the location of a supposed nest of Bolsheviks when a veteran leftist, Jim Fowler, had owned it and lived there when it was upwards of 15 units.

Keller invited me over for a personal tour of the house as we swapped stories about the building and the North Side. Soon thereafter, I arranged to have one of my walking tours gather there. On the heels of this, Keller informed me he was running for the Colorado House of Representatives. His district included part of Capitol Hill. Not only did I give him a copy of my book on the area so he would better know that section, but I agreed to talk about the political history of the enclave at a fundraiser he held at the Capitol Hill Mansion, a bed and breakfast in the district at 12th Avenue and Pennsylvania Street. When Keller was upset in the primary, I congratulated him, telling him that, given the wacky world of politics, he was better off staying out of the legislature.

Since then, Walter has allowed me to have occasional programs and booksignings at the Lumber Baron Inn while I have usually had a tour gather there annually. On this basis, seeing that a book on the bed and breakfast would advertise its wide-ranging activities, he approached me about writing this volume to share his experiences in renovating the Mouat Mansion. He has paid me for the effort.

The text is mine. In places, such as the general overview of Potter Highlands and North Denver, I have drawn on my other writing, especially *North Side Story*. Keller readily shared stories and information with me, providing me access to files he has gathered about the mansion, the John Mouat family, Jim Fowler, and the evolution of the Lumber Baron Inn. He further reviewed the text, calling my attention to questionable assertions and providing me with new perspectives. He acted as photo editor, especially emphasizing shots of the mansion and murder mysteries, while insisting on blurry images supposedly showing ghosts. Personally, I believe such shots and the operations of ghost hunters are balderdash.

Wally Ginn of the North Side Alumni Room has been a pillar of support. Besides opening his collections to me, he has met with me for regular dinners, reflecting on his diverse experiences, including his sweeping knowledge of North Denver and Denver Public Schools. He has shared stories about Keller as a star North High student and told me about how Keller received a college scholarship from the Masons.

Jim Peiker of the Castle Marne has been a ready source of information about the character of the city's bed and breakfast industry. Carl Schmidt of the Capitol Hill Mansion has further added his knowledge and experiences in the field. In a set of chats in the early 1990s, Chuck Hillestad reflected on how he came to create the city's first modern bed and breakfast, the Queen Anne Inn.

Tom Torgove has given me steady moral support, especially assisting with photography. Sonja Leonard has arranged for her real estate firm of Leonard Leonard & Associates to publicize my books and tours on her company's web site. Holly Brooks of Capitol Hill Books has similarly assisted in seeing that my books have been well circulated and marketed. Shalisha Hammond has promoted my tours on Facebook. Laura Givens helped me grasp the mystery dinner dimension of the Lumber Baron Inn. Dinah Land and Maxine Lankford have been faithful, eagle-eyed proofreaders. All those who have come on my tours and read my books also deserve thanks for keeping me going as a local historian.

Standard histories of 19th-century Denver spell out of the origins of Highland and the doings of William Larimer. In particular, see William B. Vickers, *History of the City of Denver* (Chicago: O. L. Baskin & Company, 1880), Jerome Smiley, *History of Denver* (Denver: *Denver Times*, 1901), Stephen Leonard and Tom Noel. *Denver: Mining Camp to Metropolis* (Niwot: University Press of Colorado, 1990), and my *Denver from the Bottom Up* (Denver: New Social Publications, 2003). I touch on Denver geography in *Denver Streets: Names, Numbers, Locations, Logic* (Denver: New Social Publications, 1994).

Ruth Eloise Wiberg, *Rediscovering Northwest Denver* (Denver: Northwest Denver Books, 1976), stresses the difference between Highland and the Highlands. This is the pioneering work on the neighborhood. It talks about John Mouat and his house, 102–03, though it does not probe Potter Highlands. The latter is the subject of Diane Wilk, *The Potter–Highlands Historic District* (Denver: Historic Denver, 1997). Maud Lucinda Stevens, *A Century of Baptist Faith, 1864–1964* (Denver: First Baptist, 1963), 2–4, emphasizes the role of Walter McDuffie Potter in building the Denver church. In the late 1980s, the Potter Highlands Preservation Association issued *A Self-Guided Tour of the Potter Highlands Historic District*. Its newsletter included bits and pieces on the people who have lived there. There are copies of the latter in both the collection on the area at the Lumber Baron Inn and the North Side Alumni Center.

Thomas J. Noel mentions Potter Highlands in *Denver Landmarks & Historic Districts* (Niwot: University Press of Colorado, 1996), 94, 104. The Denver Landmark Preservation Commission has a bulky file on the area. Other looks at North Denver include R. Laurie and Thomas H. Simmons, *Highlands Neighborhood* (Denver: Front Range Research Associates, 1995); Mark A. Barnhouse, *Northwest Denver* (Charleston, SC: Arcadia, 2012), and Langdon Morris, *Denver Landmarks* (Denver: Cleworth, 1979), 93–111. Most of all, there is my *North Side Story* (Denver: New Social Publications, 2011).

After he lost his fortune, John Mouat mostly disappeared from sight. There were scattered articles on him and his business in 19th-century newspapers. *Rocky Mountain News* (*RMN*), March 10, 1889, p. 2, for example, listed his views on the eight-hour day. *RMN*, March 21, 1885, p. 8, and March 29, 1885, p. 4, looked at his company, reporting its incorporation. Also see *RMN*, July 26, 1885, p. 5. *Denver Times*, July 6, 1899, p. 2, and July 7, 1899, p. 6, told of the liquidation of the firm and Hallack & Howard's takeover of its facilities. *City of Denver*, an 1893 promotion brochure, featured Mouat Lumber. *Side by Side* (Denver: Witter Cofield Historic District, 1995), 159, emphasizes the Mouat Lumber Company Re-Subdivision. Nancy L. Widmann, *Alamo Placita Historic District* (Denver: Alamo Placita Neighbors Association, 1999), plate 1, has a confused discussion of John Mouat in the Alamo Placita neighborhood.

Members of the Mouat family have occasionally talked with Walter Keller, providing the Lumber Baron Inn with information about the family. James Jeffries of the Western History/Genealogy Department of Denver Public Library (DPL) discussed Scottish immigrants and the Shetland Islands. Others at DPL have been likewise most helpful in probing the lives and deaths of people associated with the Mouat Mansion. Other than some receipts and invoices from John Mouat Lumber Company in the Cyrus G. Richardson Papers, WH 347, the library does not have any specific holdings on Mouat.

Denver Post (*DP*), January 24, 1940, p. 2, reviewed the career of Jason Reed. Building permits at DPL and an abstract on 2543 West 37th Avenue, in the Lumber Baron Inn papers, trace the history of both that property and early land ownership on lot three of block two of Potter Highlands. There were bits and pieces about Denver Business University in *Highland Chief* during the early 20th century, esp. July 18, 1908. *RMN*, May 16, 1940, had an obituary of Hiram Fowler. DPL has only two issues of *Western Miner*, both dating from before the period when Fowler published the journal. City and business directories have assorted mentions of him and his enterprises. The 1920, 1930, and 1940 censuses list the residents at 2555 West 37th Avenue and their relationships to Hiram Fowler.

There were looks at the rise of community gardens in *DP*, March 28, 1975, p. 35, March 23, 1976, p. 36, *RMN*, May 4, 1975, *Straight Creek Journal*, May 10, 1979, p. 5, and *Up the Creek*, April 8, 1983, p. 14. *DP*, August 13, 1977, p. 12AA, profiled Jim Fowler's role in them.

A fond obituary of the gardener was Jim Winter, "Jim Fowler—A Remembrance," *Westword*, April 22, 1982, p. 3. John Hand recalled him in a 1998 discussion. The Winter 1982 catalog of Denver Free University, p. 24, also observed the passing of the instructor. Previous catalogs had listed the work of the Center for Biological Self-Sufficiency, complete with short biographical portraits of Fowler.

Rob Prince reflected on Fowler and the local Communist Party in discussions in 1999–2000. Denver Urban Gardens issues a newsletter, *The Underground News*. It says nothing about the radical origins of the program. My *From Soup Lines to the Front Lines* (Denver: New Social Publications, 2007), 276–81, 314, and *Denver in Our Time* (Denver: New Social Publications, 1999), 425–31, deal with Fowler and the role of the Communist Party in Denver.

Essentially, the story of the Lumber Baron Inn and the Keller family is based on stories of Walter Keller. He has accumulated files about the bed and breakfast, complete with numerous clippings on it. There is a limited amount about Keller at the North Side Alumni Center.

Charlie Brown Hershey, *Colorado College, 1874–1949* (Colorado Springs: Denton, 1952), is the story of the early years of that school. Also see Michael McGiffert, *The Higher Learning in Colorado* (Denver: Sage, 1964), 12–14, 17, 18, 22, 34–35, 125, 128, 143–44, 181–82. Walter Gerash shared his memories of Rudy Schware in assorted conversations. *Schware* v. *New Mexico Board of Bar Examiners*, 353 US 232, is the Supreme Court decision allowing Schware to take the bar exam. The *North Denver Tribune* has had many articles heralding the Lumber Baron Inn. It featured the impending marriage of Walter and Julie on March 16, 2006.

On March 17, 2013, Dave Cole talked about the reconstruction of the Mouat Mansion and Walter Keller's wide-ranging activities. Eve Tallon has given me a neighbor's perspective on the place. Joel Judd chatted about his family, Colonel Keller, and the 2002 legislative race on April 6 and August 11, 2013. On September 4, 2013, Steve Leonard recalled his service on the Landmark Commission and the body's dealings with the Lumber Baron Inn. Maxine Lankford shared her knowledge about Keller's first wife. Rita Montero recalled the fights over Sandoval School and the activism of Maureen Keller in informal discussions in 2010–11. Krys Kingston reflected on the quality of the construction at the Lumber Baron Inn on September 9, 2013.

The *Post* and *News* had articles from October 13 to October 16, 1970, on the murders of Cara Knoche and Marianne Weaver. *DP*, October 10, 2005, p. 1L, featured a retrospection on the homicides as a cold case. It further hinted at ghosts in the mansion. Sandy Arno Lyons, *Colorado's Most Haunted* (n.p.: SkateRight Publishing, 2011), 57–70, is typical of the trite, sensational, and rather shallow writing about ghosts at the inn.

Gene Lowall tells the story of Spider Man in Lee Casey, ed., *Denver Murders* (New York: Duell, Sloan & Pearce, 1946), chap. 8. My *Seamy Side of Denver* (Denver: New Social Publications, 1993), 147–48, 153, touches on the event. Material on Celebrity Lanes derives from my *Haunts of Washington Park* (Denver: New Social Publications, 2009), 239–41.

Index

General Index